52 Weekly S_ _ About Canada

—— Grades 4-5 ——

Written by Ruth Solski

The 52 stories in this book have been designed to familiarize and develop student awareness in Canadian Historical Sites, Famous Historical Canadian Men, Famous Historical Canadian Women, Famous Canadian Athletes, Famous Canadian Inventors and Inventions, Famous Canadian Animals, Famous Canadian Attractions and Famous Canadian Festivals. Each section contains non-fiction stories and follow-ups designed to review, strengthen, and expand students' reading and language skills while familiarizing them with different aspects of Canada. The materials in this book can be used in a variety of ways.

RUTH SOLSKI was an educator for 30 years. She has written many educational resources and is the founder of S&S Learning Materials. As a writer, her main goal is to provide teachers with a useful tool that they can implement in their classrooms to bring the joy of learning to children.

Published in Canada by:
On The Mark Press
Belleville, Ontario
www.onthemarkpress.com

Funded by the Government of Canada
Finacé par le gouvernement du Canada | Canada

At A Glance

Learning Expectations

	Canadian Historical Sites	Famous Historical Canadian Men	Famous Historical Canadian Women	Famous Canadian Athletes	Famous Canadian Inventors and Inventions	Famous Canadian Animals	Famous Canadian Attractions	Famous Canadian Festivals
Reading Skills:								
Recalling Details, Events / Information	•	•	•	•	•	•	•	•
Cause and Effect	•	•	•	•		•		
Expressing an Opinion / Ideas	•	•	•	•			•	•
Classifying Information	•	•		•			•	
Sequential Ordering		•	•		•		•	
Brainstorming				•				
Locating Information / Finding Proof		•	•	•			•	
Context Clues			•		•			
Making Inferences						•		
Language Skills:								
Kinds of Nouns / Pronouns	•	•	•	•	•			
Kinds of Verbs / Verb Tenses	•	•		•	•			
Kinds of Sentences	•	•					•	
Subject / Predicate / Object		•	•			•	•	
Adjectives / Adverbs / Phrases		•	•		•		•	
Phrases / Prepositions		•		•	•		•	
Parts of Speech				•	•	•	•	
Paragraph Writing								•
Prefixes / Suffixes		•						
Capitalization / Punctuation							•	
Singular / Plural / Possessive Nouns				•				
Conjunctions							•	
Vocabulary Skills:								
Antonyms / Synonyms / Homonyms	•	•	•	•			•	•
Word Meanings / Spelling	•	•	•	•		•	•	•
Singular / Plural / Possessive Words		•		•				•
Suffixes / Prefixes		•			•			
Syllabication		•	•	•	•			
Root Words / Compound Words		•	•	•	•	•	•	
Vowels / Vowel Combinations			•	•			•	
Alphabetical Order			•					
Blends, Digraphs					•			

SSR1135 ISBN: 9781771589659
© On The Mark Press

TABLE OF CONTENTS

SSR1135 ISBN: 9781771589659

© On The Mark Press

TEACHING OBJECTIVES

STUDENTS WILL:

- read and become more knowledgeable with different aspects of their country such as Canadian Historical Sites; Famous Historical Male Canadians; Famous Historical Canadian Women; Famous Canadian Athletes; Famous Canadian Inventors and Inventions; Famous Canadian Animals; Famous Canadian Attractions; and Famous Canadian Festivals.
- practise and review reading, vocabulary, and language skills during an informal learning experience.
- use previously learned word attack skills to unlock new vocabulary.
- practise reading and discussing information in a group situation.
- strengthen research skills using non-fiction materials.
- work independently while reading a non-fiction story and completing a follow-up activity worksheet.
- practise and strengthen written ideas, opinions, and thoughts.

TEACHING STRATEGIES:

The nonfiction stories and follow-up worksheets may be used in any of the following situations.

1. Independent Reading with Follow-up Activity: Reproduce the story sheet and worksheet for the students to use to practise their reading skills at school or for home study.

2. Reproduce each story and worksheet. Mount the information story on one side of stiff cardboard and the worksheet on the back of the same card. Laminate the cards for longer usage. The cards could be placed in boxes labelled with the name of each section. Example: Canadian Historical Sites; Famous Historical Male Canadians; Famous Historical Canadian Women; Famous Canadian Athletes; Famous Canadian Inventors and Inventions; Famous Canadian Animals; Famous Canadian Attractions; and Famous Canadian Festivals.

3. Each story could be used as a teaching tool for the entire class or for small groups. Make an overhead of the story or show it on a white board. The students could read the story silently. Any new words in the story could be discussed and word attack skills should be applied by the students to figure them out. Discuss the story's content and have the students locate and read the sentences that answer the questions while applying research and comprehension skills

4. Display the worksheet for the story on the overhead or a white board. The students could record the answers in a notebook or record the answers on the white board or discuss them orally.

5. While the story is displayed, practise students' oral reading. This could be done with a group or the entire class. Direct the students' fluency and speed with your hand or a pointer. Practise reading the story several times. Reading orally is like singing. It has its own rhythm, speed, and expression.

6. If you feel that your students will have difficulty with any of the words in the story, record them on a chart, white board or chalkboard and discuss them prior to the reading of the story. Encourage the usage of word attack skills. Ask any of the following questions:

    •   How does the word begin and end?

    •   Are there any vowels or vowel combinations inside the word?

    •   Is it a compound word?

    •   Does it look like another word that you know?

    •   Do the words in the rest of the sentence give you any clues?

7. Some of the stories could be used during social studies lessons and geography lessons.

8. Many of the stories about Canada could be used during indoor recesses as an oral activity for fun.

9. The stories could also be used with students who are experiencing reading difficulties and are placed in higher grade levels.

10. They could also be used with students or adults learning to read English.

11. Any story and follow-up activity can be reproduced and sent home as homework to strengthen the reading ability of a student.

12. The information cards could be mounted and laminated and used to develop various teacher-directed research skills.

13. Stories in one section could be reproduced with their follow-up sheets to make individual books for students to practise their reading skills.

SSR1135 ISBN: 9781771589659
© On The Mark Press

L'Anse Aux Meadows
A UNESCO World Heritage Site

The Viking Trail is a long paved highway that begins at Deer Lake and ends in St. Anthony. It is a 415 km highway that travels to L'Anse Aux Meadows, an early Viking Settlement found at the northern tip of Newfoundland/Labrador.

L'Anse Aux Meadows was discovered in 1960 by a Norwegian explorer Helge Ingstad. A citizen, of the small fishing village called L'Anse Aux Meadows, led Ingstad to a group of mounds near the village that the villagers called the 'old Indian camp.' These lumps were covered with grass and looked like the remains of houses. Ingstad and his wife Anne Stine carried out seven excavations from 1961 to 1968. They found eight complete house sites as well as the remains of a ninth.

The Norse settlement at L'Anse Aux Meadows was dated to have been built 1000 years ago between 990-1050. The buildings were believed to have been constructed of sod placed over a wooden frame and were used as dwellings or workshops. Each dwelling had several rooms. Many artifacts were unearthed such as nails, bone sewing needles, and a cloak pin.

Today, at L'Anse Aux Meadows, you can visit the only Viking site in North America. It is a UNESCO World Heritage Site. At this sight you can visit an interpretation centre where you can watch a 30 minute movie about the site's history. Then you can look at the artifacts that have been found and the reconstructed scenes from Viking Times.

Outside the centre is a trail that leads to the ankle-high remains of some workshops and dwellings. While standing at this site one can think about and imagine what life was like in Viking days. Then one can visit the reconstructed village buildings and watch people dressed in Viking costumes perform and demonstrate the Viking way of life and how things were made by them.

On the beach at L'Anse Aux Meadows you could view a Viking ship named after the first European child known to have been born in North America. This ship is called the 'Knarr' and it is 16 metres long. It is a long, handmade craft of wood and iron rivets and looks like a Norse merchant ship. This craft was brought from Greenland by a crew of nine.

In the spring one can see ice bergs floating by on the ocean while you dine at a local restaurant on elk, lobster or cod and have drinks filled with chunks of ice from ice bergs. Whale watching on a viking ship would also be an exciting event.

SSR1135   ISBN: 9781771589659
© On The Mark Press

L'Anse Aux Meadows
A UNESCO World Heritage Site

A READING
Locate the answers to the following questions.

1. What is L'Anse Aux Meadows? _____

_____

2. Where is L'Anse Aux Meadows located? _____

_____

3. Who discovered the remains of this Viking settlement? _____

_____

_____

4. How were the early buildings constructed? _____

_____

_____

5. What remains of the first Viking village at L'Anse Aux Meadows? ___

_____

_____

6. How is the story of this Viking settlement told to visitors? _____

_____

_____

_____

7. What is the 'Knarr?' _____

_____

B LANGUAGE
Rewrite each sentence placing capital letters on the proper nouns.

1. In 1960 l'anse aux meadows was discovered by helge instade and his wife anne stine helge from norway.

_____

_____

2. The knarr is a 16 metre norse merchant ship that was built in greenland and brought to l'anse aux meadows by a crew of nine.

_____

_____

C WORD STUDY
Skim through the story to locate synonyms for the words below.

1. found _____   5. pretend _____

2. built _____   6. rebuilt _____

3. houses _____   7. show _____

4. path _____   8. boat _____

SKILLS: Recalling Details | Proper Nouns | Synonyms   SSR1135 ISBN: 9781771589659
© On The Mark Press

Dawson City, Yukon
Home of the Gold Rush Days

Dawson City is located on the east bank of the Yukon River at the mouth of the Klondike River. During its earlier days, Dawson City was used by the Tr"ondëk Hurëch'in First Nation People. They travelled throughout their territory harvesting salmon from the Yukon River and hunting caribou and moose in the area. They had a First Nation camp in the same place where Dawson City sits today.

This area was quickly transformed when gold was discovered in the Yukon in 1896. Dawson City was the centre of the Klondyke Gold Rush. The town was founded by Joseph Ladue and was named after a famous Canadian geologist George M. Dawson who had explored and mapped the region in 1887. It was the Yukon's capital city for many years.

During the Gold Rush, Dawson City became a thriving city of 40 000 people by 1898. In 1899, the gold rush had ended and its population fell to 8 000 people. In 1902, with only a population of 5 000, Dawson was incorporated as a city. After World War II, the Alaskan Highway was built but it bypassed Dawson City and went south to Whitehorse. In 1953, Whitehorse replaced it as the Yukon's territorial capital city. During the 1960's and 1970's Dawson City's population dropped to the 600 to 900 mark.

In the 1950's, Dawson City was linked by a road to Alaska and in 1955 with a road to Whitehorse that now forms the Klondike Highway. Since then the population has increased. The high price of gold has made modern mining operations profitable and the tourism industry has grown. The City of Dawson and the nearby ghost town of Forty Mile are featured often in the novels and short stories of author Jack London who wrote 'Call of the Wild.' Robert Service wrote many poems and stories about its people and the territory.

Dawson City has a subarctic climate. The average temperature in the summer is 15.7°C and in the winter it is -40°C. Its annual snowfall is 166.5 cm and its rainfall in July is 49.0 mm.

Dawson City's main industries are tourism and gold mining. There are eight National Historic Sites located in the city. Many of the buildings have been restored and colourfully painted. You can visit Canada's oldest gambling casino called Diamond Tooth Gertie's Gambling Hall named after a famous dance hall queen with a diamond wedged between her two front teeth. On Author's Avenue there is the Jack London Museum and the cabin of Robert Service to see. At the Palace Grand Theatre there are shows to watch from the Klondyke Days. The SS Keno is a restored paddle-wheeler that is a museum on the banks of the Yukon River. It represents the method people used for travelling to Dawson City from Whitehorse.

There are so many other interesting places to visit such as walking trails that lead to historic creeks, gold rush camps and beautiful views of Dawson City.

SSR1135   ISBN: 9781771589659
© On The Mark Press

Dawson City, Yukon
Home of Canada's Gold Rush Days

A READING

Locate the answers to the following questions.

1. What caused the change in the Tr'ondëk Hurëch'in First Nation People's lifestyle? _____

_____

_____

2. Who caused the change in their lifestyle and how? _____

_____

_____

3. When was gold discovered in the Yukon and what did this discovery bring? _____

_____

_____

4. What caused the decline in Dawson City's population in 1899? _____

_____

_____

5. What caused Whitehorse to become the Yukon Territory's capital city? _____

_____

_____

6. Why has Dawson City's population grown since the 1950's? _____

_____

_____

_____

7. List the interesting places tourists can visit in and around Dawson City. _____

_____

_____

_____

B LANGUAGE

A "collective noun" is a special noun that names groups (things) made of members (usually people). In the group of words below underline the collective nouns.

people	person	children	team	place	poems
choir	single	dozen	family	price	army

C WORD STUDY

Locate the antonyms in the story for the following words.

1. west _____

2. later _____

3. slowly _____

4. unknown _____

5. began _____

6. decreased _____

7. youngest _____

8. ugly _____

SSR1135 ISBN: 9781771589659
© On The Mark Press

Fort Macleod
Home of the North West Mounted Police

Fort Macleod is the oldest town in Alberta with a very colourful history. It is located on the Oldman River 165 km south of Calgary and one hour north of the United States border.

On May 23, in 1874, the North West Mounted Police were created by the government to bring law and order to the Alberta and Manitoba regions. When they arrived in the town, they began building a fort on an island on the Oldman River. The fort was named after Colonel James Macleod who led the first troope of officers across the prairies. The fort was used as a N.W.M.P. outpost as well as the main trading centre for Southern Alberta. Later the fort had to be moved from the island. The land was too low and the fort was often flooded. The N.W.M.P moved it to higher ground where it still sits today in the town of Fort Macleod. Over a period of time the N.W.M.P wiped out the whiskey trade in the southern plains and the town was also the scene of several famous trials.

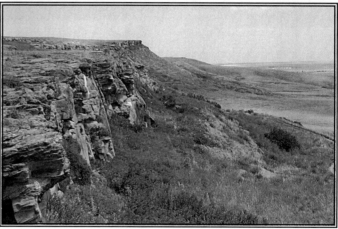

Visiting the town of Fort Macleod will transport visitors back in time. Fort Macleod is the only Designated Historic Area in the province of Alberta. This area has 60 restored buildings that were built in 1878 and the early 1900s. Fort Macleod is part of this historic Main Street. Its high walls and towers made of wood can be easily seen.

Inside the fort, people can view historical exhibits and displays of the N.W.M.P. and the First Nation People dating back to 1874. At that time, Fort Macleod was the main headquarters for the police for all of western Canada. The Fort Museum of the N.W.M.P. has artifacts, clothing, photos, and exhibits telling the history of the Mounties. The Blackfoot Gallery in the fort tells the story of the First Nation People in the area.

You can also climb the towers at the fort and walk around the fence surrounding the museum on the catwalks built a long time ago. They squeak and are scary but the view of the river, town and the museum are worth the effort.

Only 18 km from the town is a UNESCO World Heritage Site which features 'Head-Smashed-in-Buffalo Jump.' Many years ago First Nation People of the Plains drove large herds of buffalo off the 11 metre high cliff to kill them for food and their hides. At a nearby camp, the buffalo carcasses were processed. The buffalo carcass was used for tools made from the bones, the hides were used for dwellings and clothing, and the meat was used for food.

This site is named after a young Blackfoot who wanted to watch the buffalo plunge off the cliff from below. Unfortunately he was buried beneath the falling buffalo. Later he was found dead with a smashed in head. Hence the translated name Head-Smashed-In-Buffalo Jump.

A wonderful way to see and learn about life in the western provinces!

Fort Macleod
Home of the North West Mounted Police

A READING

What information does each statement give you about Fort Macleod. Record the correct words under each sentence. Does it tell who, where, what, why, when, or how?

1. Fort Macleod is a town located on the Oldman River near the United States border.

   _____

2. The government sent the N.W.M.P. to Manitoba and Alberta to bring law and order to the regions.

   _____

3. Fort Macleod had to be moved to higher ground because it was being flooded on the low land of the island.

   _____

4. Years ago the First Nation People living in the area would drive large herds of buffalo over an eleven metre high cliff to kill them.

   _____

5. Colonel James Macleod led N.W.M.P. officers across the prairies to build a fort at Fort MacLeod.

   _____

6. The buffalo hides were used for dwellings and clothing, the bones for tools, and the meat for eating by the First Nation People.

   _____

B LANGUAGE

Classify the following nouns on the chart.

visitors	dwellings	Fort Macleod	town	Alberta	troupe	river
government	police	Calgary	family	class	Blackfoot	fort
Manitoba	buffalo	museum	cliff	group	herds	island

Common Nouns	Proper Nouns	Collective Nouns
_____	_____	_____
_____	_____	_____
_____	_____	_____
_____	_____	_____
_____	_____	_____
_____	_____	_____

C WORD STUDY

Skim through the story to locate a homonym for each of the following words.

1. our   _____
2. lead   _____
3. mane   _____
4. thyme   _____
5. planes _____

6. seen   _____
7. would   _____
8. sight   _____
9. maid   _____
10. meet   _____

SSR1135 ISBN: 9781771589659
© On The Mark Press

Pier 21
Canada's National Museum of Immigration

Imagine, being a child in 1945, boarding an ocean liner with your mother in England that is heading for a port in Canada to get away from a war that has been raging for six years. There are several hundred other mothers and their children travelling aboard the ship as well. Many of the women are British and are married to Canadian soldiers. They will be travelling for a week-long trip across the frigid Atlantic Ocean. This trip is being done secretly because German U-boats patrol the North Atlantic Ocean waiting to torpedo unprotected passenger ships. When they reach Halifax's Pier 21, they disembark with all the other passengers

The passengers are taken inside Pier 21 and must sit and wait on benches to be processed by the Canadian Immigration Officials. After waiting for an entire day the little girl and her mother are processed and then taken to a train heading for Toronto by a Red Cross Worker. When they arrive in Toronto they are welcomed by her father's family.

Pier 21 operated as an ocean liner terminal and immigration shed from 1928 to 1971. It was the main point of entry for over one million immigrants and refugees from Europe and other countries. It was also a departure point for 496 000 military personel and Canadian troops during World War II. It was often called 'The Gateway to Canada.'

Pier 21 was a welcoming sight to the immigrants. It was brightly lit with many windows, highly polished floors, and benches to sit and wait on. Pier 21 was a group of buildings that contained a waiting room, a restaurant-dining room, a canteen where people could buy supplies for their train trip, a nursery, a hospital, a detention centre, a kitchen, dormitories, and a walkway overlooking the harbour.

Many times officials had to deal with immigrants that brought food such as wines, pepperoni, salami, and cheeses from their native lands. Most of the food had spoiled during the trip on board the ship and it smelled terrible. One time, officials noticed a man sitting on a bench with a towel rolled up on his lap. No one would sit on the bench near the man. Officials discovered the towel contained a dried up octopus that had decayed.

Today, Pier 21 is an immigration museum and a National Historic Site of Canada. It was closed in 1971 as immigrants chose to travel on jet airliners instead of ocean-going-ships. At the museum, visitors will find 2 000 stories, 500 oral history interviews, 700 donated books, 300 films and thousands of historical photos and scans of immigration and World War II documents and newspaper articles.

There is also a memorial called the 'Wheel of Conscience.' It is in memory of the German passenger liner MS St. Louis's 1939 voyage from Europe to North America. The 900 Jewish passengers fleeing from the Holocaust were not allowed to enter North American ports due to Antisemitism in Canada and the United States. This memorial is a polished, stainless steel wheel with four words engraved on it that caused the passengers to be turned away. The words are 'antisemitism, xenophobia, racism, and hatred.'

SSR1135 ISBN: 9781771589659
© On The Mark Press

Pier 21
Canada's National Museum of Immigration

A **READING**

Complete the following exercises.

1. Give three good reasons why you think immigrants leave their country and come to live in Canada.

_____

_____

2. List the feelings an immigrant might feel while sitting on a bench waiting to be processed.

_____

_____

3. Why were trips on passenger ships kept secret at one time.

_____

_____

4. List some problems immigrants would face coming to a new land.

_____

_____

5. How do you feel about the treatment received by the Jewish people at Pier 21?

_____

_____

6. How do you feel about Pier 21 being made into a museum? Was it a good idea or was it a waste of time and money?

_____

_____

_____

B **LANGUAGE**

Locate verbs in the story that match these meanings.

1. getting on a ship   _____
2. going from one place to another _____
3. gone bad, rotten   _____
4. found out   _____

5. running away   _____
6. rotted   _____
7. getting off a ship   _____
8. checked, inspected _____

C **WORD STUDY**

Locate the meanings of the four words on the "Wheel of Conscience" in the dictionary. Record the meanings beside the words.

1. antisemitism: _____

_____

2. xenophobia: _____

_____

3. racism: _____

_____

4. hatred: _____

_____

SSR1135 ISBN: 9781771589659
© On The Mark Press

Louis Riel (1844-1885)

Hero With a Cause

Louis Riel was born in 1844 in a community called the Red River Settlement in a territory called Rupert's Land which was run by the Hudson Bay Company. This settlement was mainly lived in by First Nation tribes and the Métis. The Métis were a mixture of Cree, Ojibwa, Saulteaux, French Canadian, Scottish and of English descent. Riel was a well-educated, intelligent, and religious young man who strongly believed like his father that the Métis had the right to protect their lands from the government.

On his return from Montreal in 1867, Riel discovered that the Métis and the First Nation people were annoyed with the number of English Protestant settlers moving into their territory. Riel also discovered that the Hudson Bay Company was planning to sell control of the territory called Rupert's Land to Canada and Ottawa was going to take it over without asking the people who lived there how they felt about the idea.

When government surveyors turned up in August of 1869 and began to stake out land that belonged to the people, the Métis settlers became very upset. They were afraid that they were going to lose their land and farms. Riel knew something must be done. He led a protest that stopped the surveyors and set up a temporary government. Sir John A. MacDonald, Canada's Prime Minister, sent his newly appointed lieutenant-governor, William McDougall, to a place called Pembina, just south of the Canadian border. Riel sent McDougall a message and warned him not to enter the Red River Territory without its government's permission. Then Riel and his followers captured Fort Gary which was the Hudson Bay's Headquarters peacefully.

On December 1, 1869, Riel presented members of his group with his plans for a new bilingual government and a list of rights that would have to be protected before the territory joined Canada. The Prime Minister sent McDougall a message to stop the takeover but he never received it in time. He had already sent one of the surveyors north to organize a militia and attack Riel and his forces. Riel learned of these plans and captured and held the men prisoners before they could attack.

The next year the Red River Settlement Committee voted to set up its own government and have Louis Riel as president. Riel made it quite clear that this area would join Canada only as an independent province, not as a controlled-by-Ottawa territory. In 1870, Riel's new government charged a violent, prejudiced man from Ontario named Thomas Scott with treason. Scott was found guilty and sentenced to death. Although Riel voted against Scott's sentence, his death would follow him for the rest of his life.

In May of 1870, Parliament passed a bill to make the Red River Settlement Canada's newest province called Manitoba. Riel had won but he had also lost as well. Troops were sent to bring peace but those from Ontario wanted revenge and treated the Métis badly. Pardons promised for Riel and other leaders were cancelled. Ontario put up a $5000 reward for Riel for having Scott executed.

Riel became a hunted man and had to hide out in the United States or Québec until 1884. Gabriel Dumont, a famous buffalo hunter and Métis leader, travelled to the United States to ask Riel to return to Canada. Dumont told Riel the same thing that happened in Manitoba was happening all over again further west and the Métis and Plains Indians needed his help. Riel packed up his family and headed home.

With Riel as the leader of this new govenment, Ottawa sent extra North West Mounted Police forces to Regina. Forts were captured and battles were fought so Ottawa sent more soldiers. In May of 1885, the final battle took place at Batouche. Dumonts' men were outnumbered and defeated. Dumont managed to escape but on May 15 Riel turned himself in. Riel was tried for treason and found guilty. On November 16, 1885 Riel was hung. The founder of Manitoba was then taken by train to St. Boniface to be buried. Great sadness hung over the entire province.

SSR1135 ISBN: 9781771589659
© On The Mark Press

Louis Riel (1844-1885)

Hero With a Cause

A READING
Complete the following activities.

1. What right did Louis Riel strongly feel the Métis had? _____

_____

Do you agree or disagree with Louis Riel? Explain why. _____

_____

2. What did Riel discover when he returned to the Red River Settlement? _____

_____

3. How did Riel try to solve these problems? _____

_____

4. Why couldn't the government stop Riel? _____

_____

5. Tell how Louis Riel won and lost his battle with the government. _____

_____

6. Why did Gabriel Dumont locate Riel in the United States and ask him to come back to Canada?

_____

_____

7. What happened at Batouche? _____

_____

8. What happened when Louis Riel turned himself in? _____

_____

By hanging Riel, what did he become? _____

_____

B LANGUAGE
Underline the verb in each sentence. Classify the verbs in each sentence as present tense or past tense.

1. Riel talked about the problem with others.   _____
2. The Métis knew there were problems.   _____
3. Please begin to survey the land.   _____
4. The government wants to buy the land.   _____

C WORD STUDY
Write the plural form of each singular word.

1. territory _____
2. land _____
3. buffalo _____
4. life _____
5. family _____
6. community _____
7. idea _____
8. hero _____

SKILLS: Fact/Opinion | Classifying Verb Tenses | Singular/Plural Words

SSR1135   ISBN: 9781771589659
© On The Mark Press

Billy Bishop (1894 - 1956)
Canada's World War I Flying Ace

On February 8, 1894, Billy Bishop was born in Owen Sound, Ontario. He was the second son of William A. and Margaret Bishop. As a child growing up his parents had no idea of how famous Billy would become. He did not do well in his school studies and preferred outdoor activities such as hunting and riding. One day after reading about the first airplane to be built in Canada, Billy decided to build his own. Using cardboard, wooden crates and string, Billy created a plane and took it to the roof of his family's three-storey home and tried to fly it. Unfortunately he crashed onto the ground and was rescued from the wreckage by his sister.

At the age of seventeen, Billy decided to follow in his older brother's footsteps and attend The Royal Military College in Kingston, Ontario. His parents hoped the school's discipline would help to improve his studies but unfortunately it did not happen. During his third year in 1914, Billy was nearly expelled for stealing a canoe to sneak into Kingston to meet some girls. In the same year he was caught cheating on his exams. Feeling certain that he would be expelled for his bad behaviour, he decided to join the army since World War I had broken out in Europe. In September he enlisted and was assigned to a Toronto cavalry unit. Although Billy went to war on horseback, which was the oldest method of fighting wars, he would soon be introduced to a much more modern weapon - the airplane!

Bishop and other members of the cavalry travelled to Ireland on a cattle ship and ended up in the horrible trenches filled with a mixture of mud and manure. Bishop hated his situation. One day while suffering in the stench and mud of the trenches during a storm, there suddenly appeared a shiny object buzzing in the sky. It was an airplane! Bishop then decided that he wanted to meet the enemy in the air not in the stinking, muddy trenches.

Bishop began his flying career as an observer. His excellent vision helped him spot enemy formations on the ground and in directing bombs towards them. In 1916, Bishop's luck changed when he met an influential woman who knew his father in Canada. She helped Bishop to attend an air-training school.

During this war, fighter pilots were not expected to have a long life. They were often shot down in their first three weeks as a pilot. Fortunately for Bishop he survived this dangerous career. In 1917, Bishop forced five German observation balloons out of the sky which cleared the way for Canadian troops who attacked Vimy Ridge on April 9. In the months of April and May, Bishop shot down more than twenty planes. One of his most courageous feats took place on June 2, 1917. Alone, he attacked a German airfield early in the morning and ambushed seven planes.

Bishop's fearless style of flying at the front of the pack while leading his pilots over enemy territory made him realize that he could easily be shot down. After one patrol, a mechanic counted 210 bullet holes in his aircraft. His new method of surprise and his blue-nosed aircraft was noticed by the Germans who referred to him as 'Hell's Handmaiden' and 'the greatest English scouting ace.'

By the end of World War I, Bishop claimed he had 72 air victories. He was rewarded with various awards and medals for his bravery such as the Victoria Cross, Distinguished Service Order, the Military Cross and the Distinguished Flying Cross.

It has been said many times that Billy Bishop had the most difficult type of courage, 'the courage of the early morning.'

SSR1135   ISBN: 9781771589659
© On The Mark Press

Billy Bishop (1894-1956)
Canada's World War I Flying Ace

A   READING
Tell why each event took place in Billy Bishop's life.

1. Billy's sister had to rescue Billy one day because _____

_____

2. Billy did not do well at school because   _____

_____

3. Billy's parents were pleased that Billy wanted to attend the Royal Military College because _____

_____

_____

4. Billy Bishop decided to enlist in the army because _____

_____

5. Bishop wanted to learn how to fly because _____

_____

6. Bishop was extremely courageous on June 21 in 1917 because _____

_____

7. Fighter pilots were not expected to have a long life because _____

_____

8. Bishop was an excellent observer during flights because _____

_____

B   LANGUAGE
There are four kinds of sentences: Assertive, Interrogative, Imperative, and Exclamatory. Record the name of each type on the line.

1. "I'm going to build my own plane!" shouted Billy. _____

2. The men found the trenches muddy and smelly. _____

3. How many medals did Billy Bishop receive during World War I? _____

4. "Shoot!" screamed the pilot to the gunner when he saw the German plane. _____

C   WORD STUDY
Record the plural form for each of the singular words.

1. activity _____   5. enemy _____

2. bullet _____   6. member _____

3. trench _____   7. victory _____

4. study _____   8. bomb _____

SKILLS: Cause and Effect | Kinds of Sentences | Plurals   SSR1135   ISBN: 9781771589659
© On The Mark Press

Timothy Eaton (1834-1907)
Canada's Famous Entrepreneur

No one would have ever thought that a young Irish boy, who grew up on a properous farm in Ireland, would be the founder of the largest chain of Canadian stores and a mail-order catalog business in Canada.

Timothy Eaton never saw his father, John Eaton, as he died before Timothy was born. His mother was a clever, independent woman and with the help of her eight older children kept the farm running for the first years of Timothy's life. Unfortunately in 1846, the potato famine had struck Ireland. Two of Timothy's brothers and three of his sisters emigrated to Canada as they knew the farm could not feed and support all of the family.

At the age of fourteen, Timothy acquired his first taste of running a business when he began to work as a shopkeeper's apprentice in a nearby town. The shop sold a wide variety of goods from clothing to medicine. Timothy worked many long hours from four in the morning until after midnight. He was always exhausted and often slept under one of the counters instead of going home. Although the work was long and tiring, Timothy learned a great deal about running and stocking a store. At the end of his apprenticeship, Timothy at the age of nineteen, wearing a new suit with 100 pounds ($12 000) in one of the pockets boarded a ship to Canada. When he landed in Canada, he worked on his sister's farm but soon found another job working as a clerk and bookkeeper in a general store.

In 1860, in the town of St. Mary's, Timothy and his two brothers opened up a dry goods store that sold fabric, clothing, and groceries. Business in those days was done by haggling and bargaining as goods did not have an affixed price. Timothy was not in favour of buying and selling goods in this manner. He felt goods should have a fixed price. Margaret, his wife, knew he was unhappy and encouraged him to open a store in Toronto. On a cold, freezing morning on December 8 in 1869, the first T. Eaton Co. Limited store was opened for business in a small shop at 178 Yonge Street in Toronto. Three employees and Eaton himself served the customers. An advertisement that Eaton had placed in the Toronto Globe promoted customer interest. The ad stated that the store only sold their goods for cash and there would only be one price for each item. There would be no bargaining. The ad also stated if the goods were not satisfactory the customer's money would be refunded. Hundreds of people flocked to his store after seeing the ad.

In 1883, Eaton opened another larger store farther north on Yonge Street as he now had competition from another merchant, a Scottish immigrant by the name of Robert Simpson, who had opened a store near Eatons. In 1884, the T. Eaton Company published a mail-order catalog so customers in all parts of Canada could order goods from the store. The first Eaton catalog had no pictures and was 32 pages long. By the 1900's, the catalog was thick and well illustrated. It was often referred to as the 'wishing book' or the 'Farmer's Bible.' Timothy Eaton cared for his employees and their hard work. He closed his stores earlier than his competitors and gave his employees Saturday afternoon off during the summers so they could have fun with their families. He often helped those who were sick and needy. He was a strict father and did not believe in smoking, drinking, and card playing. His stores never sold tobacco products or playing cards.

In 1907, Timothy Eaton, one of Canada's greatest businessmen, died of pneumonia. Because he was an avid churchgoer and donated money frequently to the Trinity Methodist Church, his family had the Timothy Eaton Memorial Church built in his memory. At the Royal Ontario Museum sits a bronze statue of Timothy Eaton given by his employees to the Eaton family for all their help during World War I. At one time, this statue sat in one of the Eaton stores close to the Queen Street doors. Timothy's left shoe gradually lost its bronze look as people often touched it as they exited through the doors. Unfortunately there are no longer any Eaton stores in Canada as shopping methods and heavy competition changed the retail market. Many Canadians will never forget Timothy Eaton and shopping at his stores or looking through his spring, fall, and Christmas catalogs.

Timothy Eaton (1834-1907)
Canada's Famous Entrepreneur

A READING

Complete the following activities.

1. List the ways in which Timothy Eaton developed strong business skills.

_____

_____

_____

_____

_____

2. Timothy Eaton had some strong feelings about certain bad habits. Tell how he honoured these beliefs.

_____

_____

3. In what ways did Timothy Eaton show how he cared for his employees.

_____

_____

_____

4. How do you think Timothy Eaton would feel today if he could see how his business was destroyed?

_____

_____

5. Think of ways that shopping for goods have changed over the years.

_____

_____

B LANGUAGE

A sentence is made of a subject and predicate. Example: (Mr. Eaton) announced the store will be closed on Saturday afternoons during the summer. In each sentence below circle the subject and underline the predicate.

1. Timothy Eaton worked as a shopkeeper's apprentice.
2. Timothy and his brothers opened up a dry goods store.
3. Robert Simpson became Timothy Eaton's competitor.
4. Hundreds of people flocked to the new T. Eaton store.

C WORD STUDY

Match the words below to their meanings.

clever   emigrate   haggling   donated   famine   support   promoted   exhausted

1. bargaining   _____

2. settle   _____

3. very tired   _____

4. given away   _____

5. time of starving   _____

6. smart, intelligent   _____

7. to hold up   _____

8. raised up   _____

SSR1135   ISBN: 9781771589659
© On The Mark Press

Sir John A. Macdonald (1815-1891)
First Prime Minister of Canada

John Alexander Macdonald was born in Glasgow, Scotland on January 11 in 1815. He was the third of five children of Helen and Hugh Mcdonald. His father's many failed business ventures caused the family to immigrate to Kingston in Upper Canada in 1820. His family lived over the store that his father ran. When this business failed his family moved to Hay Bay west of Kingston and his father was given a new job as a magistrate.

John attended local schools and when his parents had enough money he was sent to Midland Grammar School in Kingston. At 15, he was finished with school as his parents could not afford to send him to university. They decided he should become a lawyer and Macdonald knew he needed money to help support his family as his father's businesses were failing again. John Macdonald grew up not having any boyhood and at the age of 15, he was employed as an apprentice lawyer with George Mackenzie, a prominent lawyer, in Kingston.

Highlights of Sir John A. Macdonald's Political Career

- elected as a municipal alderman in Kingston, Ontario in 1843.

- was a member of the Legislative Assembly of the Province of Canada from 1844 to 1867.

- appointed Receiver General or Treasurer of the Province of Canada in 1847.

- was an opposition member of parliament from 1847 to 1854.

- helped to create the Conservative Party in 1854.

- was Attorney General of Canada West for 12 years and looked after law and order in the country.

- served as Joint Premier of the province of Canada with Étienne-Paschal Tiche for two years and George Étienne Cartier for five years.

- sat as an Opposition member of parliament in 1858 to 1864.

- attended all three conferences on Canadian Confederation and was responsible for writing most of the B.N.A. Act

- was knighted by Queen Victoria and was asked to become the first Prime Minister of Canada in 1867.

- during the building of the Pacific Railway there was a huge scandal and Sir John A. Macdonald had to resign as Prime Minister in 1873.

- in 1878, he became Prime Minister again and during this period of time the Pacific Railroad was completed.

- Sir John A. Macdonald won three more elections in 1882, 1887, and 1891

- unfortunately three months after his 1891 election, Sir John A. Macdonald died.

Sir John A. Macdonald's accomplishments as Prime Minister were incredible. Two very important accomplishments were completed during his years as Prime Minister. They were the building of the Canadian Pacific Railway and Confederation which linked Canada as a country from coast to coast.

Thanks for a job well done Sir John A.! We do have a great country!

SSR1135 ISBN: 9781771589659
© On The Mark Press

Sir John A. Macdonald (1815-1891)
First Prime Minister of Canada

A READING

Record the date(s) when Sir John A. Macdonald held the following positions or completed the following accomplishments.

1. _____ • had to resign as Prime Minister of Canada.

2. _____ • was an opposition member of parliament.

3. _____ • helped to create the conservative party.

4. _____ • won three more elections as Prime Minister.

5. _____ • appointed Receiver General or Treasurer of the Province of Canada.

6. _____ • was knighted and asked to be Canada's first Prime Minister.

7. _____ • died three months after his election.

8. _____ • elected as a municipal alderman in Kingston.

B LANGUAGE

Divide the subject and predicate of each sentence with a vertical line. Put one line under the bare subject and two lines under the bare predicate.

1. John A. Macdonald lived in Glasgow, Scotland.

2. His father ran a store.

3. John needed money for his family.

4. Queen Victoria knighted John A. Macdonald in 1873.

C WORD STUDY

Use a dictionary to find and record the meaning for each of the following words. Use each word in a good sentence.

1. apprentice: _____

_____

_____

2. magistrate: _____

_____

_____

3. scandal: _____

_____

_____

4. confederation: _____

_____

_____

5. opposition: _____

_____

_____

SSR1135   ISBN: 9781771589659
© On The Mark Press

Robert Samuel McLaughlin (1871-1972)
Businessman and Philanthropist

Who would have thought that a large automobile business would have developed from a blacksmith shop in the village of Enniskillen about 20 km from Oshawa, Ontario?

Sam McLaughlin was born on September 8, 1871 and he was the youngest son of Robert McLaughlin who owned the McLaughlin carriage works which was the largest manufacturer of horse drawn buggies and sleighs in the British Empire.

Some interesting Trivia Facts to read about Sam McLaughlin:

- The carriage company grew and had to be moved to a larger community of Oshawa in 1876. It was called the McLaughlin Carriage Company of Canada Limited in 1901. By 1915, the company was making one carriage every ten minutes.

- When Sam was 16, he completed high school and apprenticed in his father's carriage works and became a journeyman. For a few years Sam worked in Watertown, Syracuse, and Binghamton in New York State so he could gain more experience and knowledge in the industry.

- On Sam's 21st birthday, his father announced that Sam and his older brother George would be made partners in the carriage company with him.

- Sam was named the chief designer for all McLaughlin carriages and sleighs.

- The development of motor cars caught Sam's attention and he decided to design a line of vehicles.

- At first, Sam's father was reluctant but finally Sam and George persuaded him about the future of the car and he gave in.

- The McLaughlin Motor Car Company was established with Sam as its president.

- The company's first motor car was not truly an original and this attempt failed.

- Then Sam McLaughlin and William C. Durant, who owned the Buick Motor Company, made an agreement to work together building cars. The cars were called 'McLaughlins' or 'McLaughlin-Buicks.' The name depended on how well they sold.

- In 1918, Sam McLaughlin put his two companies called the McLaughlin Car Company of Canada and the Chevrolet Car Company of Canada together as one. By doing this General Motors of Canada was born.

- Sam McLaughlin was a generous business man who donated large amounts of money to the University of Toronto and the McLaughlin Planetarium near the Royal Ontario Museum. To the city of Oshawa he gave money for the Oshawa Public Library, the McLaughlin Art Gallery, Camp Samac, Lakeview Park, and the Oshawa General Hospital as well as many other institutions in the province.

- The McLaughlin Estate called Parkwood is now used for tours, weddings, parties, television movies and shows.

- Sam McLaughlin will always be fondly remembered as Colonel Sam by the 34th Ontario Regiment as he helped to pay salaries of some of the regiments' soldiers when the government funding was stopped.

Robert Samuel McLaughlin (1871-1972)
Businessman and Philantropist

A READING

Record the correct ending for each sentence.

1. Robert McLaughlin who owned the McLaughlin Carriage Works was _____

_____

2. Sam McLaughlin was Robert McLaughlin's _____

_____

3. In 1876, the carriage company had to be _____

_____

4. In 1915, the carriage company could make _____

_____

5. Sam's surprise birthday gift from his father made _____

_____

6. Sam became interested in _____

_____

7. General Motors was created when _____

_____

8. Sam McLaughlin was a generous business man to the city of Oshawa because _____

_____

_____

_____

B LANGUAGE

A phrase is a group of words that begins with a preposition. It describes how something looks or moves. Underline the phrases in each sentence.

1. Each vehicle required fifteen coats of paint.

2. Sam McLaughlin loved to ride his horses and to compete in many show-jumping competitions.

3. In 1934, his colt called 'Harometer' was the winner of the Queen's Plate.

4. Sam McLaughlin's love of horses led to the building of Parkwood Stables a few miles from Oshawa.

C WORD STUDY

Add the suffixes 's, ed, ing' to each verb. Watch the endings of the words for changes.

1. experience   _____   _____   _____

2. announce   _____   _____   _____

3. develop   _____   _____   _____

4. manufacture   _____   _____   _____

5. design   _____   _____   _____

6. complete   _____   _____   _____

SSR1135   ISBN: 9781771589659
© On The Mark Press

Josiah Henson (1789-1883)
Hero of Uncle Tom's Cabin

While growing up on an American farm or plantation, many young slave children witnessed extremely cruel acts and punishments handed out by white masters and cruel overseers. Josiah Henson was one of those children. He saw the wounds on his father's back after he had been whipped and noticed he was also missing one of his ears. Josiah's father had been punished because he tried to prevent his wife from a terrible attack by the overseer. Later his father was sent away and Josiah's family never saw him again. His mother and her six children were sent back to their original owner, a doctor. When the doctor died, his property had to be sold which included the slaves. Josiah's family was going to be split apart but his mother begged her new owner to let Josiah come with her. The buyer agreed and never regretted his decision.

Josiah grew up to be one of his strongest, smartest, and most faithful workers. In time Riley, the owner of the farm, put Josiah in charge of it. While in charge, Josiah always set aside some of the crops harvested so the slaves would be well fed. When Josiah was 18, he became involved with a local church and loved the messages that he heard about love and hope. Later, he became a Christian and began to preach these same messages to his own people. Josiah developed strong feelings about the unfairness and cruelty of slavery. At the age of 20, Josiah was badly beaten by another slave owner's overseer. His arm was broken and his shoulder blades were so badly smashed that they couldn't be set properly and never healed correctly. For the rest of Josiah's life, he could never raise his arms above his head.

At the age of 22, Josiah met and married a young, slave girl named Charlotte. They had a long and happy marriage with twelve children. In 1825, the Henson family ran into problems with their owner Riley. It was then that Josiah decided to escape with his family and head to Canada. Late one night in 1830, with only a small parcel of food, twenty-five cents, and the clothes on their backs, the Henson family left the plantation one moonless night. The youngest child was carried by her father in a pack on his back. During the day they hid quietly in a safe spot from the slave catchers. During the night they carefully and quietly moved through thick forests and mucky swamps using the North Star to guide them. The Henson family travelled in this manner for six weeks until someone from the Underground Railroad helped them to reach safety in Upper Canada. When Josiah crossed the bridge over the Niagara River he fell to his knees and kissed the ground.

In 1842, Josiah helped to establish an all Black Settlement called 'Dawn' near Dresden, Upper Canada. This settlement provided a new beginning for Black American refugees. It had a brickyard, a grist mill, and a sawmill. One very important building was an industrial training school which helped to teach and train the people in the many skills they needed in order to survive.

Henson also told an author 'Harriet Beecher Stowe' stories about his life as a slave and the brutal ways he and other slaves had been treated by their owners. These stories were told in her book called 'Uncle Tom's Cabin' which was published in 1852 and sold 300,000 copies the first year that it was published. This book made people realize how badly Black American Slaves had been treated.

Josiah Henson led the way in trying to change the attitudes of many people which helped to develop a more muticultural attitude in North America's society.

SSR1135   ISBN: 9781771589659
© On The Mark Press
 Image credit: rook76 / Shutterstock.com

Josiah Henson (1789-1883)

Hero of Uncle Tom's Cabin

A READING
Complete the following activities.

1. List ways that black slaves were treated on American farms and plantations years ago.

_____

_____

_____

_____

2. Why was Josiah treated better than most slaves by his owner? _____

_____

_____

3. How did getting involved with the local church change Josiah?

_____

_____

4. Why do you think Josiah escaped to Canada with his family? _____

_____

5. How did Josiah Henson help black refugees who had escaped from slavery?

_____

_____

_____

6. How did Harriet Beecher Stowe help black American slaves?

_____

B LANGUAGE
Underline the adverbs and circle the verbs in each sentence.

1. Josiah was badly beaten by a cruel overseer.
2. His shoulder blades could not be set correctly and never healed properly.
3. During the day the family hid quietly in a safe spot so slave catchers would not see them.
4. At night the Henson family moved silently and carefully through the forests and swamps.

C WORD STUDY
Classify each pair of words as homonyms, antonyms or synonyms.

1. strong, weak _____
2. realize, understand _____
3. witnessed, watched _____
4. kind, cruel _____
5. parcel, package _____

6. scent, cent, sent _____
7. planted, harvested _____
8. heel, heal _____
9. guide, lead _____
10. manner, way _____

SKILLS: Recalling Events and Details | Adverbs | Antonyms/Synonyms   SSR1135   ISBN: 9781771589659
© On The Mark Press

Walter Rolling (1873-1943)
An Early Black Educator

Walter Rolling was born on May 31 in 1873 in a small town called Laskay. His father, Benjamin Rolling Junior was a pedlar, storekeeper, and post master in the town. Walter attended the Strange School as a boy. It was the closest school to the town but Walter still had a quarter mile walk twice a day.

Walter was an outstanding student who was taught by the same teacher throughout public school. He was able to attend the Aurora High School in 1892. Very few students enrolled in high school because they had to pay four dollars for each term. Most students who finished high school at that time chose teaching as a career. Walter Rolling earned his Third Class Teaching Certificate from the Newmarket Model School.

Walter's first teaching position was at a school in Aurora. The class that he was to teach was a difficult group who were hard to control. They had already embarrassed and humiliated a woman teacher by trying to take off her clothes. The woman teacher left town very upset. The principal of the school greeted Rolling at the door of the school. He asked Rolling if he had brought a club with him. Rolling was very shocked when he heard the question. The principal took him aside and gave him a wooden spoke that came out of a wagon wheel. Rolling quietly slipped it inside the sleeve of his coat.

At first, the students did try to get away with some of their tricks but Rolling showed them that he meant business and was in charge by waving and banging the wheel spoke during his first eight days. Once the students realized that he meant what he said, Rolling had no trouble at all. When Rolling was assigned to another school his reputation preceded him and he found the students were afraid of him.

In January of 1895, Rolling began to teach at Kinghorn School which was a one-room schoolhouse. His first year's salary was $295.00 and he had to do other jobs to survive. Even though he was offered a senior teaching position in 1910 which paid more money, Rolling turned it down because he really enjoyed teaching at Kinghorn.

Rolling also showed a keen interest in sports in the community. He was involved in many children's sports and coached the Kinghorn Girls Baseball team. He himself enjoyed playing football and was one of the players on the Newmarket Football team in 1893 when they won the district championship.

Rolling offered a class at the school which was the same as grade nine for the students who were not able to go to Aurora for high school. Students came from miles around to attend his class as it was not offered anywhere else nearby.

For thirty years of teaching, Walter Rolling never had a student fail in his class. He was a strict teacher but also a fair one. He would rather reason with a student than use the strap. He always tried to instill in his pupils the idea that the students and the teacher must work together in order to gain respect.

Walter Rolling was presented with a gold watch when he retired from teaching on June 30, 1936. The next year, the community honoured his teaching and dedication to the community on June 16, 1937 and called it 'Walter Rolling Day.' On this day more than 2 000 people attended including the Minister of Education.

Walter Rolling was a well respected man, educator, and a friend of little children!

SSR1135 ISBN: 9781771589659
© On The Mark Press

Walter Rolling (1878-1943)
An Early Black Educator

A READING

Does the sentence describe learning in the 'present' or the 'past?' Record the correct word on the line.

1. Students who live far from their school travel to it by bus. _____

2. One teacher taught all eight grades in a one room school. _____

3. Schools are large and contain many different rooms. _____

4. Students had to walk along muddy roads carrying their books and lunch boxes to school. _____

5. Students who want to become teachers must attend university after high school. _____

6. Highschools and elementary schools have many teachers and students. _____

7. A teacher's salary for the year was $600.00. _____

8. Students are not punished with a strap or made to stand in the corner. _____

9. Students and teachers should work together to gain respect for each other. _____

10. Many students could not go to high school because they could not afford the fees. _____

B LANGUAGE

A 'preposition' is always the first word in a phrase. Complete each sentence using 'prepositions.'

1. Walter Rolling was able _____ attend the high school _____ Aurora.

2. Students had _____ pay four dollars _____ each high school term.

3. Walter Rolling taught _____ a school _____ the country.

4. Walter Rolling walked _____ the classroom filled _____ difficult children holding a wheel

   spoke _____ his sleeve.

C WORD STUDY

Divide the following words into syllables

1. attended _____   5. presented _____

2. position _____   6. survive _____

3. principal _____   7. community _____

4. reputation _____   8. preceded _____

SSR1135   ISBN: 9781771589659
© On The Mark Press

John Ware (1845-1905)
A Famous African-North American Cowboy

John Ware was a famous African-North American cowboy who was well-known and respected for his ability to ride and train horses. He was also famous for driving large herds of cattle to southern Alberta in 1882 which helped to create the ranching industry in the province.

John Ware was born and raised as a slave on a cotton plantation in South Carolina in the United States. After the southern states lost the Civil War all black slaves were set free. Always wanting to be a cowboy, John Ware headed for the state of Texas to learn the skills of a rancher and to become one. While living in Texas, Ware was employed to drive large herds of cattle northward along the Western Cattle Trail to northern territories.

In 1882, Ware was hired to help bring 3 000 head of cattle from the United States to a ranch called The Bar U in the foothills southwest of Calgary, Alberta. Here Ware found that experienced cowboys were in great demand in this northern territory. He decided to stay and worked for several cattle companies. He also worked for the Bar U and Quorn ranches. At the Quorn ranch, Ware was put in charge of a large herd of wild horses.

Many stories and legends have been told about John Ware's impressive physical strength, good nature, and great courage. He would walk fearlessly over the backs of cattle in pens and could stop a steer head-on and wrestle it to the ground. His remarkable strength helped him to break the wildest horses or he could trip a horse by hand and hold it on its back to be shod. Ware could easily pick up a young steer and throw it onto its back to be branded.

In 1890, Ware started his own ranch on the Sheep River near Millarville and in 1892 he married Mildred Lewis, who came with her family from Toronto, Ontario and they had six children. In 1900, John Ware decided to move to a new ranch site along the Deer River east of Brooks. The first home on this ranch was destroyed by a spring flood in 1902. Ware built their second home on higher ground overlooking a stream called Ware Creek. Unfortunately the family did not live in the new home for long. In 1905, Ware's wife, Mildred, died in April and John was killed when his horse tripped in a badger hole and fell on him in September of the same year.

John Ware was a remarkable man. His good nature, amazing strength, good sense of humour, and his courage gained him immense respect from all the people in Alberta. It is indeed an amazing feat how he successfully, as a Black man, established himself in a white european society in the 19th century Canada.

Alberta has honoured this legendary cowboy by naming places after him such as Mount Ware, Ware Creek, John Ware Ridge, John Ware Junior High School to name a few. John Ware's family log cabin was carefully restored and relocated and now sits in Red Deer Valley in Dinosaur Provincial Park for all to see and visit.

John Ware is one of Alberta's legendary people.

SSR1135   ISBN: 9781771589659
© On The Mark Press

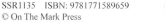

John Ware (1845-1905)
A Famous African-North American Cowboy

A READING
Number the sentences that describe John Ware's life story in the correct order.

_____ During the Civil War in the United States, the south lost and all the slaves on plantations were set free.

_____ Since John Ware had always wanted to be a cowboy he headed towards Texas to learn about ranching.

_____ On a cotton plantation in South Carolina, a young black baby named John Ware was born. He grew up as a slave and worked in the cotton fields with his parents.

_____ In 1890, Ware started his own ranch on Sheep River and in 1982 he married Mildred and they had six children.

_____ He was hired to drive large herds of cattle north along the Western Cattle Trail to northern territories.

_____ In 1902 the Ware's new home was destroyed by a spring flood and a new one was built on higher ground.

_____ One of his trail drives took him to the Bar U Ranch southwest of Calgary with 3 000 head of cattle. He liked the area and saw the need for experienced cowboys and decided to stay

_____ During 1905, John Ware and his wife Mildred died.

_____ In 1900, Ware moved his family to another ranch on Deer River because more people were moving near them.

B LANGUAGE
Underline the adjectives and adjective phrases in each sentence.

1. John Ware enjoyed driving large herds of cattle to northern territories.

2. Experienced cowboys were needed in northern ranching communities.

3. His remarkable strength helped him handle the wildest horses.

4. John Ware built the second cabin of logs on higher ground.

C WORD STUDY
Record the 'root words' for the following words.

1. respected _____

2. rancher _____

3. married _____

4. companies _____

5. fearlessly _____

6. remarkable _____

7. wildest _____

8. territories _____

9. unfortunately _____

10. carefully _____

SSR1135   ISBN: 9781771589659
© On The Mark Press

Elijah McCoy (1843-1929)
Canadian-American Black Inventor

Elijah McCoy was born in Colchester, Ontario in 1843. His parents were escaped slaves who had left Kentucky and had made it into Canada on the Underground Railroad. His father, George McCoy served in the Upper and Lower Canada Rebellion in 1837 and for his honourable service the Canadian Government gave him 160 acres of farmland near Colchester, Ontario.

When Elijah was three, his family returned to the United States and settled in Detroit, Michigan. Elijah attended public school until he was 15. His parents were able to save enough money to send him to Scotland to study mechanical engineering in 1859 to 1860. Here he served as a mechanical apprentice.

When the Civil war was over in the United States, Elijah returned to Canada. He was not able to locate a job in his field in Southwest Ontario and returned to Michigan to find work as an engineer. The Michigan Central Railroad hired him even though they could not imagine a Negro being an engineer. His job was to stoke the boiler and to lubricate the steam cylinders and sliding parts of the train.

Trains in Elijah's day were run by hot, high pressure steam which can rust most metals. In order to avoid this from happening a thin film of oil was used to protect and seal the steam cylinders and pistons. In those days trains needed to stop to be lubricated to prevent overheating. Elijah McCoy developed a lubricator for steam engines that did not require the train to be stopped. His lubricator used steam pressure to pump oil wherever it was needed.

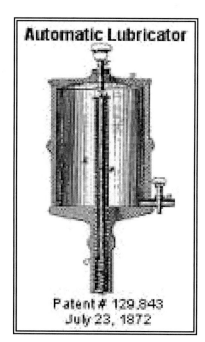

Automatic Lubricator

Patent # 129,843
July 23, 1872

Elijah patented this device in 1872 and continued to improve on his design. McCoy's new lubricators were used in the engines of railroads and shipping lines. McCoy was promoted by his employer as an instructor to teach about his inventions and how they worked. Later he became a consultant to the railroad industry on patent matters.

McCoy's lubricator was so successful that buyers, of steam trains and steam engines used in mines and factories, would ask if the lubricator used in the engine was the 'Real McCoy.'

Elijah McCoy's invention helped to develop automation which improved the work place for many factory workers.

It seems that Elijah McCoy had the last laugh on his doubtful employers!

SSR1135   ISBN: 9781771589659
© On The Mark Press

Elijah McCoy (1843-1929)
Canadian- American Black Inventor

A | READING

Explain *how* or *why* each event took place in the information story about Elijah McCoy.

1. Elijah's parents travelled on the Undergound Railway. _____

_____

2. The Canadian Government gave George McCoy 160 acres of land. _____

_____

3. Elijah McCoy was sent to Scotland in 1859. _____

_____

4. Elijah left Canada and went to live in Michigan. _____

_____

5. Elijah had to lubricate certain parts of the train. _____

_____

6. Trains had to be stopped regularly. _____

_____

7. Elijah's invention worked. _____

_____

_____

8. Elijah's employers promoted him. _____

_____

B | LANGUAGE

A word that is used instead of a noun is called a *pronoun*. Pronouns help us to speak and write the names of persons and things without repeating them. Circle each pronoun in the following sentences.

1. We escaped to Canada safely on it.

2. He went to Scotland for two years.

3. Many felt that Elijah's invention was fantastic.

4. They hired him as a train engineer.

C | WORD STUDY

A *prefix* is a syllable added to the beginning of a word. Add prefixes to the words below.

1. hook _____

2. arm _____

3. head _____

4. obey _____

5. air _____

6. turn _____

7. do _____

8. ordinary _____

SSR1135 ISBN: 9781771589659
© On The Mark Press

Lincoln Alexander (1922-2012)
A Multicultural Believer

Lincoln Alexander grew up as a child in Ontario, Canada. His parents were immigrants from the West Indies. His mother, Mae Rose, came from Jamaica and his father, Lincoln Alexander Senior, came from St. Vincent and was a porter on the Canadian Pacific Railway. Alexander was born on January 21 in 1928 and grew up to become a well-educated, prominent, Canadian citizen.

Did you know that:

- Alexander went to Earl Grey Public School and Riverdale Collegiate in Toronto.

- In 1942, Alexander joined the Royal Canadian Air Force and served as corporal until 1945 during World War II.

- After World War II, Alexander turned to higher education and earned a degree from McMaster University in 1949 and a law degree from Osgoode Hall Law School in 1953.

- Alexander practised law in Hamilton with several law firms.

- In 1965, he was appointed to Queen's Counsel and also ran as a Conservative Member of Parliament for Hamilton West but was defeated.

- Three years later on June 25, 1968 Alexander won the seat for HamiltonWest and was the first Black Canadian to sit in the House of Commons.

- Alexander was re-elected four times and served a total of 12 years from 1968 to 1980.

- In 1979, Alexander was appointed Minister of Labour in the Clarke government and held this position until 1980.

- In 1980, Alexander resigned his seat in the House of Commons as he was appointed chairman of the Workers' Compensation board. In this position he worked for five years.

- On September 20 in 1985, Lincoln Alexander was sworn in as Ontario's 24th Lieutenant-Governor and was the first Black Canadian to hold this high position.

- As Lieutenant-Governor, Alexander was able to take an active role in the multicultural affairs of Ontario. He served in this position for five years.

- Lincoln Alexander was known for his sound judgement, compassion, and humanity.

- On October 19, 2012 at the age of 90 Lincoln Alexander died. His body lay in state at Queen's Park and Hamilton's City Hall. Flags were flown at half mast on all government buildings.

- In November of 2013, the government of Ontario declared January 21 of each year to be called 'Lincoln Alexander Day.' This day is to honour a great man's outstanding service in the fight for the equal rights for all races in our Canadian society.

SSR1135 ISBN: 9781771589659
© On The Mark Press

Lincoln Alexander
A Multicultural Believer

A READING

Record the date when each event happened in Lincoln Alexander's life.

1. received a law degree from Osgoode Hall _____

2. joined the Royal Canadian Air Force _____

3. was born in Ontario _____

4. earned a degree from McMaster University _____

5. was appointed to Queen's Counsel _____

6. lost his election as a Conservative Member of Parliament _____

7. got re-elected as a Conservative Member of Parliament four times _____

8. was the first Black Canadian to become Ontario's 24th Lieutenant-Governor _____

9. the day when Lincoln Alexander's outstanding service is honoured _____

10. the government of Ontario honoured him for his services _____

11. won the seat for Hamilton West and was the first Black Canadian to sit in the House of Commons

    _____

12. resigned his seat in the House of Commons as he had a new job _____

B LANGUAGE

A sentence which contains only one subject and one predicate is called a <u>simple sentence</u>. If a sentence is made of two subjects and two predicates, it is called a compound sentence. Record the words '<u>simple</u>' or '<u>compound</u>' after each sentence.

1. Lincoln Alexander joined the Royal Canadian Airforce and he became a corporal. _____

2. Lincoln went to Earl Grey Public School. _____

3. Lincoln Alexander was Ontario's Lieutenant-Governor for five years. _____

4. Lincoln Alexander died in 2012 and his body lay in state at Queen's Park. _____

C WORD STUDY

Record the 'root word' for each of the following words.

1. compassion	_____	6. multicultural	_____
2. humanity	_____	7. education	_____
3. government	_____	8. defeated	_____
4. appointed	_____	9. judgement	_____
5. compensation	_____	10. appointed	_____

Laura (Ingersoll) Secord (1775-1868)
A Woman of Courage

Laura (Ingersoll) Secord was born on September 13, 1775 in the United States. She was the daughter and oldest child of Thomas and Elizabeth Ingersoll. Laura grew up during the War of Independence between Britain and the United States. She did not have a happy childhood and had to bear the responsibility of caring for her younger siblings when her mother died.

After the America War of Independence, Thomas Ingersoll heard that Canada was offering settlers free land in Upper Canada (Ontario) so he decided to move his family to Queenston. Here he opened a tavern to make money so his family could settle on the land near Ingersoll on the Thames River. In this same area the Secord family also settled after the war so they could remain loyal to Britain. Laura Ingersoll and James Secord met, fell in love, and married sometime in the later 1790s. At first, they lived on a farm but James was not happy being a farmer and preferred to be a merchant and to have his own store. They moved back to Queenston where James opened a store.

In 1812, the United States declared war on Britain and they began attacking forts and towns around Niagara. It was than that James decided to join the militia. During the war, a horrible battle took place at Queenston Heights and James Secord was one of the injured men. Laura was told by a passing soldier that James was injured and she ran to get him to bring him home. When Laura and James returned to their house they found that it had been vandalized during the battle. Laura decided to take James to relatives where their children were staying.

In June, of the following year, the Secords returned to their home in Queenston but they found that things were not any better. James was still too weak to work and nearby Fort Geroge had been taken over by the Americans. One day, Laura was shocked to find American soldiers standing at her door demanding food. While the soldiers were eating, Laura overheard their plans. She was horrified when she heard that 500 soldiers were on their way to make a sneak attack on fifty British soldiers led by Lieutenant James Fitzgibbon. The attack was to take place on June 23 and it was already June 21. Laura realized that she had two days to warn Lieutenant Fitzgibbon. She knew that Fitzgibbon and his men were camped near Beaver Dams (now Thorold, Ontario) about 20 km away. Laura knew that she had to go and soon.

At dawn the next day, Laura quietly rose, kissed her children good-bye, and told them that she had to go to visit their sick uncle and slipped out of the house. Laura was not afraid to be caught and questioned by any American soldiers as she had a good excuse for being on the road. Laura was hoping her sick brother-in-law would be able to ride the rest of the way with the message. Unfortunately, her brother-in-law was too ill to travel so Laura knew she had to keep on walking. Laura's niece offered to walk with her but only lasted for four hours in the hot sun and Laura had to leave her at Shipman's Corners.

Laura trudged on along back roads, across farmer's fields and through swampy land. Her route made her journey ten km longer but she wanted to avoid being caught. As the sun was setting Laura was exhausted, her arms and legs were scratched and she had lost her shoes. She still had to cross one more field and climb one last hill when suddenly she was surrounded by a group of Iroquois soldiers in the darkness. The men thought they had caught a spy but Laura was able to convince them to take her to Fitzgibbon. At first Fitzgibbon didn't know whether to believe her story because standing in front of him was an exhausted, bedraggled, dirty woman. She did not present a pretty picture. Laura was so determined that he believe her message that Fitzgibbon decided to act on her warning.

When the American forces reached Beaver Dams, they were trapped by Iroquois warriors and soldiers who made them surrender This battle was a major loss for the Americans and a major victory for Fitzgibbons who was promoted. Unfortunately, Laura Secord was not recognized for her efforts until 1860 when Prince Edward, Queen Victoria's oldest son, saw her name on a list of all the soldiers who had fought bravely for the British during the War of 1812. Noticing the name of the only woman 'veteran' on the list, the Prince decided to send her a gift of 100 pounds which was a fortune in those days.

SSR1135 ISBN: 9781771589659
© On The Mark Press
 Image credit: rook76 / Shutterstock.com

Laura (Ingersoll) Secord (1775-1868)
A Woman of Courage

A **READING**

Tell the cause and the effect of each situation in Laura Secord's life and historic adventure.

1. Laura had to care for her younger siblings.

Cause: _____

Effect: _____

2. The Ingersoll family moved to Upper Canada and Mr. Ingersoll opened a tavern.

Cause: _____

Effect: _____

3. The Secord family moved to the same area.

Cause: _____

Effect: _____

4. James Secord decided to join the militia.

Cause: _____

Effect: _____

5. Laura quietly left her home at dawn the next day.

Cause: _____

Effect: _____

6. Fitzgibbon was not sure he could believe the woman that was standing before him.

Cause: _____

Effect: _____

7. The Americans were defeated.

Cause: _____

Effect: _____

B **LANGUAGE**

Personal pronouns are words that stand for persons. Skim through the story to look for personal pronouns listed below. Put a check mark beside each one used.

☐ I   ☐ you   ☐ them   ☐ yours   ☐ me   ☐ we

☐ she   ☐ theirs   ☐ he   ☐ us   ☐ hers   ☐ mine

☐ him   ☐ they   ☐ his

C **WORD STUDY**

Complete the following words from the story with the correct r-controlled vowel sound.

ar   er   ir   or   ur

1. b____n   2. Ing____soll   3. Am___ican   4. tav____n   5. Sec____d

6. f____st   7. f____m   8. m____chant   9. st____e   10. h____rible

11. inj____ed   12. ret____ned   13. d___kness   14. warri____s   15. eff____ts

SKILLS: Cause/Effect | Personal Pronouns | R-controlled Vowel Sounds   SSR1135   ISBN: 9781771589659
© On The Mark Press

Lucy Maud Montgomery (1847-1942)
Canada's World Famous Author

Lucy Maud Montgomery made P.E.I a favourite tourist destination for thousands of people and devoted fans of her many books. L.M. Montgomery was born on November 30, 1874 in Clifton (now New London), P.E.I. and her parents were Clara Woolner Macneill and Hugh John Montgomery who came from well-established families. Unfortunately Maud's mother died before she reached the age of two. She was then sent to live with her mother's parents in Cavendish on the northern coast of the island. While growing up, Maud had no one her own age to play with and her imaginary playmates kept her company. The Macneill house contained many books and since Maud was an early reader she spent much of her time with her nose in a book reading. Although Maud spent most of her days alone she did have a happy childhood. When she was nine she began writing poetry and keeping a journal.

Maud's father lived and worked in Prince Albert, Saskatchewan as a government official and a real estate agent. When he remarried he requested that Maud, who was 16 at the time, come out west to live with him. Maud enjoyed spending time with her father and exploring this part of Canada. While Maud lived in Prince Albert, she had her first poem called 'On Cape Leforce' published in the Charlottetown Patriot, a newspaper. In June of the next year Maud had an article published in the Prince Albert Times. Even though Maud and many successes with her writings in Prince Albert she became homesick and longed to return to the island. In 1891, Maud went home and went back to school to become a teacher but still hoped to become a writer some day. While teaching school, Maud continued to write stories, articles, and poems for newspapers and magazines which gave her extra money. Unfortunately in 1898, Maud's grandfather Macneill died and Maud had to resign her teaching position to care for her grandmother Macneill. Maud spent 13 years of her life in Cavendish except for one year when she worked at the Halifax Daily Echo, a newspaper, as a writer and proofreader. During that time Maud made a good living from her writings and became one of Canada's most successful, freelance writers. After one year she returned to Cavendish to continue caring for her grandmother.

Maud indeed loved Cavendish and all of its beauty but she was lonely. She longed to have a husband and her own family. At one time while she had been teaching, Maud did meet and fall in love with a young farmer but she knew that she could never marry him as he would be socially unacceptable for her family. Later she met Ewan Macdonald, a minister. Maud did not love him but respected him on a social and intellectual level. They became secretly engaged but could not marry while her grandmother needed her. The years from 1902 to 1911, brought Maud little joy and she even questioned and resented her grandparents religious beliefs and the lack of warmth and love they had shown her. The one bright spot in her life was the writing of 'Anne of Green Gables' which brought her success and fame. The story of Anne of Green Gables began as a short serial for a girl's magazine. Maud loved the character and wanted the story to be published as a book. She sent her book to five publishers who showed no interest in publishing it. Maud was so disappointed she hid the manuscript in a hat box. A few months later, Maud took it out of the box, looked it over, made a few changes, and sent it away again. This time the publisher accepted it and suggested that she begin writing a sequel to it. In June of 1908, Maud's first book called Anne of Green Gables was published. Her readers wrote letters telling her how much they enjoyed her book and encouraged her to write more. Maud wrote more books about Anne and the last one was published in 1939.

In 1911, Maud's Grandmother Macneill died and she was finally able to marry Ewan Macdonald. After their honeymoon abroad, the Macdonalds moved to a small community of Leaskdale, Ontario. Maud found it a charming place but still preferred Cavendish. Maud and Ewan had two sons called Chester and Stuart. The role of a minister's wife and the responsibilities of a mother kept Maud's life very busy but she found time to write. She longed for Cavendish and the island but she never returned to live there.

On April 24 in 1942, Lucy Maud Montgomery passed away and finally returned to the island that she dearly loved and was buried in the Cavendish cemetery close to the site of her old home. Today, people can get close to Lucy Maud Montgomery by visiting the National Park in Cavendish to relive the stories told in her many books and feel her spirit.

SSR1135   ISBN: 9781771589659
© On The Mark Press

Lucy Maud Montgomery (1847-1942)

Canada's World Famous Author

A — READING

Complete the following activities.

1. Tell how L.M. Montgomery developed her great imagination.

   _____

   _____

2. While Maud was living in Prince Albert, she became homesick and returned to the island in 1891. Think of other reasons why she may have wanted to leave.

   _____

   _____

3. In what ways was Maud still interested in writing as an adult?

   _____

   _____

4. What event drastically changed Maud's life?

   _____

   _____

   Do you think young people in our modern society today would do the same? Tell why.

   _____

   _____

5. When did L.M. Montgomery's skills as a writer expand and get better?

   _____

   _____

6. What was the highlight of L.M. Montgomery's life during the 13 years she spent caring for her grandmother?

   _____

   _____

B — LANGUAGE

Is the underlined word in each sentence a noun, verb, adjective or adverb?

1. Imaginary playmates kept Maud company.   _____

2. Maud began writing when she was nine.   _____

3. Maud's father lived in Prince Albert.   _____

4. Maud and Ewan were secretly engaged.   _____

C — WORD STUDY

Skim through the story to find homonyms for the following words.

1. dye _____
2. scent _____
3. reel _____
4. right _____

5. bean _____
6. merry _____
7. cereal _____
8. ate _____

9. new _____
10. sight _____
11. rote _____
12. roll _____

SKILLS: Expressing an Opinion | Parts of Speech | Homonyms   SSR1135   ISBN: 9781771589659
© On The Mark Press

Molly Brant (1736-1796)
A Prominent Mohawk Loyalist

Molly Brant was born around 1736 in a Mohawk village in the Ohio River Valley. She lived with her father Peter, her mother Margaret, and her brother Joseph. When her father died the family moved back to the Mohawk River Valley in New York State. Molly's mother remarried a Dutch settler by the name of Nickus Brant who owned a farm and was a friend of Sir William Johnson, the British Superintendent for Northern Indian Affairs. Molly and her brother Joseph both used Brant as a surname. They grew up living like Europeans which was unusual during this period of time. Their home was a large colonial style frame house and they used many European household items. Molly attended a mission (religious) school where she learned to read and write in English. She was also fluent in Mohawk.

As Molly grew up she became interested in native politics. The Iroquois used a system of government based on the power of women in the family. At 18, Molly travelled with other Mohawks to Philadelphia to fight for the rights of Mohawks in some land problems. At the age of 22, Molly married the rich farmer and British Superintendent Sir William Hall who was in charge of Indian Affairs. They had eight children and lived in an elegant home called 'Johnson Hall' until 1774. They lived as wealthy, powerful people. Molly held power in her Iroquois clan but also lived well as a 'european' lady. She took care of her husband's business while he was away and controlled the servants and black slaves who worked in the house. Molly and her husband often entertained and had visitors from far-away places. In July of 1774, Sir William Hall died at the age of 59. Molly inherited a large sum of money that she used to establish a trading business.

During the American Revolution in 1775, Molly stayed in her home in Canjoharie and provided food and assistance to British Loyalists and Mohawks who were fleeing from New York to Canada. She also acted as a spy for the British military. During the same year, British forces invaded New York from Canada and laid seige of American Patriots in Fort Stanwix. Molly heard that a large group of Patriot militia was on its way to help the fort so she sent Mohawk runners to warn the British commander of the danger. At this battle, British Mohawk and Seneca forces ambushed the Patriots and their Oneida allies in the Battle of Oriskany. During this battle Iroquois warriors were fighting on both sides and the battle was a brutal one. The Oneida and the American Patriots retaliated against Molly Brant and pillaged her home in Canjoharie. She was able to escape with her children to Fort Niagara (near Niagara Falls) leaving most of her belongings behind.

Throughout the war, Molly travelled back and forth from Fort Niagara to Fort Haldeman on Carleton Island on the St. Lawrence River (near Kingston) to Montreal. The British asked her to keep the Iroquois on their side. In return, Molly became very powerful and received many gifts from the 'British Government's Indian Affairs Department.' Many Iroquois and Loyalist homes and farmlands were seized and burned by the American Patriots. Molly took care of numerous starving and poor Iroquois families who arrived at Fort Niagara from New York.

When the American Revolutionary War was over, Molly and Joseph Brant (her brother) asked Governor Haldimand for help. Land was given to Joseph Brant along the Grande River, west of Lake Ontario and to John Deserontyou on the Bay of Quinte on the St. Lawrence River in Upper Canada (near Trenton and Belleville, Ontario.

Molly Brant did not live in either place. She settled at Cataracqui (now Kingston). She was given land and a house was built for her by the army. She was also provided with clothing and money to replace the things that she had lost during the war. Molly was proud of her heritage and always dressed like a Mohawk among the European settlers and continued to help the sick and the poor Iroquois as much as she could and continued to ask the government for help. She spent the remainder of her days as a highly respected woman. In 1796, Molly died and was buried in a church graveyard in Kingston.

Molly Brant will always be remembered for her good heart and her brave deeds.

Molly Brant (1736-1796)

A Prominent Mohawk Loyalist

A READING
Complete the questions below.

1. List the reasons why Molly Brant grew up to be a strong, intelligent woman.

   _____

   _____

   _____

2. List the ways that Molly Brant was a brave woman and a risk-taker.

   _____

   _____

   _____

3. In what way was Molly Brant a humanitarian?

   _____

   _____

4. In what way did Molly Brant show others that she was proud of her heritage?

   _____

   _____

5. Give reasons why people should be proud of their own heritage and culture.

   _____

   _____

   _____

B LANGUAGE
Personal Pronouns stand for persons. Underline the personal pronoun in each sentence.

1. She lived in a Mohawk village with her parents.

2. They lived as wealthy important people.

3. The Mohawk runners were sent to warn them.

4. He was an important man in the British government.

5. I will warn them of the raid.

C WORD STUDY
Locate and record a synonym for each of the following words in the story.

1. rich   _____

2. guests   _____

3. friends   _____

4. grabbed   _____

5. many   _____

6. fight   _____

7. start   _____

8. destroyed   _____

9. differences _____

10. attacked   _____

SSR1135   ISBN: 9781771589659
© On The Mark Press

Mary Ann Shadd (1823-1893)
Educator, Abolitionist, Feminist

Mary Ann Shadd was born on October 9 in 1832 and was the oldest of 13 children. Her parents Abraham and Harriet Shadd and their family were free blacks and lived in Wilmington, Delaware in the U.S.A. The family was respectable and hard working but were also involved in a dangerous business called the Underground Railroad. They helped runaway slaves travel through slave states to areas where slavery had been abolished. In the state of Delaware, there were no schools for black children so the Shadd family moved to the state of Pennslyvania where Mary Ann could attend one. When Mary Ann completed her education she returned to Delaware and opened a school for black children. She also taught in many other schools in the north-eastern part of the United States.

In 1850, the American government passed the 'Fugitive Slave Act.' This law stated that all runaway slaves, even those living in a free state, still belonged to their slave owners and must be returned to them. The northern free states were no longer safe places for escaped blacks and free blacks to live. In Canada, slavery had been abolished for a number of years and the black people looked to Canada West (Ontario) as a safe place to live and have freedom. Thousands of slaves and free blacks escaped to Canada by using the Underground Railway. In Canada West, Henry and Mary Bibb were the leaders of the community and they invited Mary Ann Shadd to come and set up a school and teach the free black children. Mary Ann accepted their offer and came to Windsor to set up a school. The Bibbs and Mary Ann Shadd did not always agree on how black communities should live in Canada. The Bibbs believed in segregation which meant the blacks should live in closed neighbourhoods and set up their own churches and schools. Mary Ann Shadd felt black people in Canada should not be grouped together but spread out in existing communities and attend the same schools and churches with white people. She believed in integration. Mary Ann also refused to teach at a 'blacks only' school which caused hard feelings between her and the Bibbs. Mary Ann set up a private school to give black children an education because poor black communities could not get funding for public schools. Her school was open to black and white students. During the day she taught children and during the evenings adults. Her school was located in a run-down old building where during the winter Mary and her students froze while during the summer they were cooked.

Many false stories and lies were being told in the United States about life in Canada West so Mary Ann researched and wrote a 44 page booklet called 'Notes of Canada West' and had it published in 1852. The booklet contained useful information about life in Canada West, the different settlements, and how they worked. Her booklet also criticized segregated black communities. In 1853, Mary Ann began her own newspaper called 'The Provincial Freeman.' Even though she was the editor, Mary Ann hired a man and used his name so people would read her paper. Her newspaper often contained articles on racial discrimination, women's rights, and the importance of women. In order to keep her paper running, Mary Ann went on a lecture tour in the United States to make money. She spoke against slavery and encouraged black people to immigrate to Canada. In 1854, Mary Ann moved her newspaper headquarters to Toronto, in Canada West where there was a larger black population. It was here that she used her own name as the editor. Once the public discovered that M.A. Shadd was a woman they were extremely angry about a woman doing a man's job. Mary Ann was afraid the public would not buy her paper and the last black newspaper in Canada would have to close so she hired a minister as editor and moved the newspaper headquarters to Chatham.

In 1856, Mary Ann married Thomas Cary who was a hard working member of the black community and had a son and a daughter. In 1857, a depression swept across Canada West causing Mary Ann to close her newspaper. In 1865, the American Civil War had ended and slavery was finally abolished in the United States. Mary Ann returned to the United States to teach school to help educate the millions of newly freed slaves. She also became a lawyer and worked hard to get black women the right to vote. At the age of seventy, this great woman who had done so much for her people, died peacefully.

Mary Ann Shadd dedicated her life to improving the quality of life for everyone black and white, male, and female.

Mary Ann Shadd (1823 - 1893)

Educator, Abolitionist, Feminist

A READING

A. Number the events that took place in Mary Ann Shadd's life in the correct order.

_____ Henry and Mary Bibb asked Mary Ann Shad to come to Windsor in Canada West to set up a school for black children.

_____ Because people were being told lies about life in Canada, Mary Ann wrote a booklet called 'Notes of Canada' to give useful and honest information about living in Canada.

_____ Mary Ann Shadd was the first child of Abraham and Harriet Shadd and was born on October 9 in 1823. She was the oldest of 13 children.

_____ Once the people found out M.A. Shadd was a women they accused her of stealing a man's job so she moved her paper to Chatham and hired a man to be the editor.

_____ The Shadd family moved to the state of Pennsylvania so Mary Ann could attend school.

_____ When Mary Ann became a teacher in the United States she opened a school for black children.

_____ In 1853, the newspaper called the 'Provincial Freeman' was started by Mary Ann Shadd and it had articles on racial discrimination, women's rights, and the importance of women.

_____ In 1856, Mary Ann Shadd married Thomas Cary and had to close her newspaper because of a depression in Canada

_____ Once the Civil War was over in the United States and slavery had ended, Mary Ann returned to teach school to help educate the thousands of freed slaves.

_____ In 1854, Mary Ann moved her newspaper to Toronto where there was a larger black population.

B LANGUAGE

Some pronouns are used to ask questions. They are called *Interrogative Pronouns*. Record the correct Interrogative Pronoun in each sentence.

what   who   whom   whose   which

1. _____ was the Underground Railroad used for?

2. _____ travelled on the Underground Railroad?

3. _____ newspaper had articles on racial discrimination?

4. The black slave did not know _____ road was the safest to travel on.

5. With _____ did Mary Ann Shadd disagree?

C WORD STUDY

Skim through the story to locate words that have the following meanings.

1. honest and decent   _____

2. being a slave, bondage   _____

3. ended, stopped   _____

4. a person who is running away _____

5. isolating, setting apart   _____

6. home in a new country   _____

7. treated differently   _____

SSR1135   ISBN: 9781771589659
© On The Mark Press

Anna Haining (Swan) Bates (1846-1888)
Canada's Gentle Giantess

Imagine standing 2.27 metres tall when you are fully grown. Everyone around you is beneath you. Have you ever heard about a Canadian woman who stood this tall? Her name was Anna Haining (Swan) Bates and she lived in Nova Scotia.

Some interesting facts about Anna Haining (Swan) Bates:

- Anna Haining Swan was born on August 6, 1846 and weighed 8 kg (18 pounds) at her birth. She was the third child of 13 children who were of typical height and weight.

- Anna grew very quickly. At the age of four she stood 137 cm tall; at six she stood 157 cm tall and was a little smaller than her mother; at ten she stood 1.85 metres tall. On her fifteenth birthday, Anna measured 213 cm tall. Two years later Anna stood 2.2 metres (7 feet, 5 inches) in height.

- As Anna grew taller she became a tourist attraction and people would follow her through the streets of Millbrook asking her all kinds of questions.

- Once Anna was fully grown she weighed 159 kg (350 pounds) Her feet measured 34 cm (13 1/2 in.) long.

- During the 1860s, Anna was hired by P.T. Barnum owner of the large Barnum and Bailey Circus to work at his museum as the Gentle Giantess. At his museum in New York, Anna began by doing two shows a day. Anna was advertised as the only gentle giantess who was 7 feet 5 inches (2.2 metres) tall and weighed 350 pounds (159 kg.) During one of her acts in her show, Anna measured her waist with a long tape measure and then gave it to a woman in the audience to use around her waist. The woman could wrap it around her waist three times.

- One day a fire broke out in the museum and the stairs were on fire and Anna was overcome by the smoke. She was too large to escape through a window so the men who worked at the museum found a derrick nearby to smash the wall around one on the third floor. They then lowered Anna by block and tackle with 18 men holding the rope. At that time Anna weighed 179 kg.

- While visiting a circus in Halifax, Anna was spotted by the promoter and hired on the spot. At this circus Anna was paired with a very tall man by the name of Martin Van Buren Bates. They became a touring sensation, fell in love, and married. They had two children but both of them died during their birth because of their huge size.

- After touring England with the circus the Bates moved to Seville, Ohio where they bought land and had a house built to suit their size and needs. The ceilings were very high and the doorways very wide. All the furniture was specially built so they could sleep and sit comfortably.

- In 1879, the Bates toured for the last time with the circus and retired at their farm to lead a quiet life. In 1888, Anna Bates died suddenly and unexpectantly in her sleep the day before her 42nd birthday.

'Anna handled being different in a graceful, dignified way.'

Anna Haining (Swan) Bates (1846-1888)
Canada's Gentle Giantess

A READING
Using words found in the story complete each sentence.

1. Anna was _____ by the _____ of a large circus to _____ at his _____ in New York.

2. Many _____ followed Anna all over the _____ of Millbrook _____ questions.

3. Anna _____ 8 kg when she was _____ and _____ very _____ .

4. Anna's _____ was three _____ bigger than the _____ of most _____ .

5. Ann was rescued from a fire at the _____ by men who used a _____ to smash the wall around a window and then _____ her to the ground using a _____ and _____ .

6. The _____ for the Bates' new home was _____ built so they could sit and sleep _____ .

7. The Bates had two _____ but both of them _____ because of their _____ .

8. A _____ hired Anna to work with _____ as a _____ and they became a touring _____ .

B LANGUAGE
Pronouns which point out a particular person or thing are called *Demonstrative Pronouns*. Complete the sentences with the correct pronouns.

this   that   these   those

1. _____ is a great act to watch at a circus.

2. _____ very tall lady is Anna Haining Bates.

3. _____ men used _____ derrick to smash the wall around _____ window.

4. _____ woman towers above all of _____ men.

C WORD STUDY
Locate a homonym in the story for each word below.

1. way   _____

2. feat   _____

3. waste   _____

4. stares   _____

5. rap   _____

6. higher   _____

7. pared   _____

8. dyed   _____

SSR1135   ISBN: 9781771589659
© On The Mark Press

Harriet Tubman (1820-1913)
Slave, Conductor, Black Moses

Harriet Tubman was a courageous woman who rescued people from slavery. She was born a slave in 1820 in the slave state of Maryland. At the age of seven, Harriet began working as a field hand in the fields of a plantation. She spent from sunrise to sunset plowing the land, splitting wood, and cutting hay. As the slaves worked they often sang songs while the overseer watched them. The overseer felt that quiet slaves were thinking about escaping so he would force them to sing. Little did he know that the songs that they sang had hidden messages.

Harriet could not read or write as it was against the law to teach slaves these skills. Educated slaves would be able to read road signs and had a better chance of escaping. Anyone who taught slaves these skills would be imprisoned or put to death. When Harriet was fifteen, she helped another slave to escape. An angry overseer hit her with an iron weight on the head and knocked her unconscious for several days. When Harriet recovered she had a deep dent in her forehead where her skull bone had been crushed. This blow caused her to have terrible headaches and unusual sleeping spells for the rest of her life. Harriet would suddenly black out and fall asleep at any time or any place. Sometimes these spells would take place two or three times a day. She had no idea when they would have happened. As a slave, to escape and not get caught was difficult because of his or her skin colour. A slave's only hope was to escape to a free state where there was a law against slavery such as New York or Pennsylvania. Harriet often thought about escaping even though she could not read or write. Once she found out her owner planned to sell her she escaped to Pennyslvania by using the Underground Railroad. Once Harriet was settled in Philadephia, she enjoyed her freedom but was lonely and missed her family. She heard that conductors on the Undergound Railroad often returned to their plantations to rescue their families. She decided to be one and was angry when she was told only men could be conductors. She felt that since she was treated and worked like a man on the plantation and was not afraid she should be allowed to become one. Her wish was granted and she worked at several jobs to make money to buy a gun for her new career.

Harriet rescued members of her family as well as other slaves who were brave enough to endure the dangerous journey. Harriet would appear at a plantation without any warning late at night. Outside the slaves' cabins Harriet would softly sing 'When that chariot comes, who is coming with me?' The people inside the cabin would sing back 'When that old chariot comes I'm going with you.' Harriet brought food, medical supplies, and often carried people who were to weak to walk. She always had her pistol with her.

When the United States passed the law that ordered marshalls and deputies to hunt down runaway slaves in free states, Harriet decided to take escaped slaves to Canada on the Underground Railroad. She brought more than three hundred escaped slaves to Canada. Each trip was dangerous and difficult. Harriet and her passengers hid in damp cellars, under cabins, in secret rooms in houses and barns, inside hollowed out haystacks in fields, and up inside chimneys. At night they walked through thick forests and waded through icy, cold, waist-deep water to throw the dogs of slave-catchers off their scent. Harriet found her way by using the North Star or by feeling the trunks of trees for moss to discover which way was north. Harriet would not allow any of her passengers to turn back as she knew that slaves who returned to their plantations were beaten and tortured to tell what they knew about the Underground Railroad. If anyone tried to turn around and go back, Harriet would pull out her gun and say 'Dead men tell no tales. Go on or die!' Her word was law and not one of her passengers was caught. Slave owners offered large sums of money as rewards for Harriet's capture—dead or alive! They found it difficult to believe that a woman who was a slave was stealing their slaves.

When the Civil War broke out in 1861, Harriet returned to the United States and joined the Union Army. She worked as a nurse, a scout, and a spy. After the Civil War, Harriet lived in the town of Auburn, New York to be close to her friends from the Underground Railroad. Today her home is a museum.

In 1913 on March 10, the woman that many called "Moses" died at the age of 93.

SSR1135 ISBN: 9781771589659
© On The Mark Press

Harriet Tubman (1820-1913)
Slave, Conductor, Black Moses

A READING
Answer the following questions.

1. In what way were the slaves able to communicate and give messages even though they could not read or write? _____

   _____

2. What did Harriet suffer from even though she could not recall them happening?

   _____

   _____

3. In what ways was Harriet Tubman a brave, courageous woman? Record three ways.

   _____

   _____

   _____

4. How did Harriet communicate with the slaves she was going to help escape?

   _____

   _____

5. How did the slaves respond to her question? _____

   _____

6. Why do you think Harriet did not tell the slaves when she planned to rescue them?

   _____

   _____

7. Why do you think slave owners found it difficult to believe that a black female slave was stealing their slaves?

   _____

   _____

B LANGUAGE
Pronouns which stand for no particular person or thing are called *Indefinite Pronouns*. Complete each sentence with the correct indefinite pronoun in the box.

some	few	others	each	one

1. _____ escaped safely.

2. She always cared for the safety of _____.

3. _____ died on the trip to Canada

4. _____ knew how badly slaves were treated.

5. _____ came to Canada with only their clothes.

C WORD STUDY
Circle the words that might describe the feelings felt by a slave while escaping.

afraid	peaceful	insecure	brave	irritated	frightened	unsafe	relaxed	content
calm	nervous	happy	jumpy	peaceful	unsure	worried	secure	cautious

SKILLS: Recalling Details | Indefinite Pronouns | Descriptive Words

SSR1135 ISBN: 9781771589659
© On The Mark Press

Emily Pauline Johnson (1861-1913)
Poet, Writer, Mohawk Princess

On March 10, in 1861 on the Six Nations Reserve near Brantford, Ontario, George and Emily Johnson's fourth child was born. They named her Emily Pauline but she was always called Pauline. George Johnson was a well-educated Mohawk and spoke many languages. When he married Emily Susannah Howells, who was English, he went against his parents wishes and Iroquois traditions. According to the traditions of his people the child of a white woman could never be a chief of a nation.

George Johnson built a beautiful mansion called 'Chiefswood' on the Six Nations Reserve for his English bride. It was here in this elegant home that Pauline and her siblings lived in luxury and met many important people from all over the world. Pauline was taught by a governess for two years then attended the reserve school and later a highschool in Brantford. After her schooling, Pauline lived the life of a rich young lady attending parties, plays, and writing her poetry. Unfortunately her lifestyle changed when her father died and left the family with very little money. Chiefwoods, their home, was closed up and Pauline, her sister, and her mother had to rent an apartment in Brantford. Her brothers had jobs and could care for themselves. Pauline and her sister Eva tried to get jobs but years ago there were not many for women. Eva did get an office job but Pauline hoped to earn money writing and selling her poetry. During her lifetime Pauline made no more than 500 dollars for her poems.

In 1892, Pauline was invited to take part in a concert to read her poetry. It was here that she realized she had a talent for reciting her poetry dramatically as the audience responded with clapping and cheering after her performance. Pauline began giving recitals. Since there were no radios, movies or television in the late 1800s people depended on touring performers who entertained them in schools, saloons, tents, and church halls.

Pauline's tours took her all across Canada and this is when her love for her country grew with a passion. During her performances Pauline talked about First Nation communities that she had visited and how beautiful and magnificent Canada was. Audiences loved and admired her thrilling and unforgetable readings. Her fame spread quickly and Pauline became the leading platform entertainer in Canada.

Pauline's recitals even took her to London, England. She recited her poetry in high society homes and theatres. While performing she wore traditional clothing worn by a Mohawk woman. Her colourfully fringed and beaded buckskin dress, her beaded moccasins and a bear-claw necklace made quite an impression on British people who had never been to North America. Her performances and poetry described Canada's nature and the experiences of First Nation People.

Travelling from place to place was often difficult as it was done by train or horse and cart. Pauline found that she had little time to read or write. In 1909, she decided to retire in Vancouver, British Columbia and to focus on her writing. She began by writing stories told to her by a Squamish chief and had them published in a Vancouver newspaper. In 1911, Pauline discovered she had breast cancer and became too weak to write. Her friends secretly arranged to have her beautiful Squamish stories published in book form. Over twelve thousand copies of her book called 'Legends of Vancouver' were sold and the money was used to support her during her painful illness.

Pauline Johnson died at the age of 51 and people across Canada morned the loss. Flags in Vancouver flew at half-mast and huge crowds attended her funeral. Pauline's ashes were buried in beautiful Stanley Park in Vancouver on March 10, 1913 which was a very appropriate place for a nature lover to rest in peace.

Pauline Johnson was proud of her Mohawk heritage and loved Canada's nature.

Emily Pauline Johnson (1861-1913)
Poet, Writer, Mohawk Princess

A READING
Answer the following questions.

1. Describe the lifestyle of the Johnson family while they lived in Chiefswood.

   _____

   _____

2.. Describe Pauline's lifestyle after she finished all of her schooling. _____

   _____

3. What changed the lifestyle of the Johnsons and how did it affect the family? _____

   _____

4. What event changed Pauline's career? _____

   _____

5. Why was the life of a performer difficult in the late 1800s? _____

   _____

6. Why do you think people in England would be impressed with Pauline's performances? _____

   _____

   _____

7. How did the people in Canada show their respect for a great poet? _____

   _____

   _____

B LANGUAGE
Classify the pronouns using the correct terms: Personal   Interrogative   Demonstrative   Indefinite

1. several   _____
2. they   _____
3. this   _____
4. some   _____
5. which   _____

6. mine   _____
7. who   _____
8. those   _____
9. either   _____
10. yours   _____

C WORD STUDY
Record the root word for each of the following words.

1. parties   _____
2. writing   _____
3. governess   _____
4. performers   _____
5. impression   _____

6. poetry   _____
7. copies   _____
8. clapping   _____
9. reciting   _____
10. unforgetable   _____

SSR1135   ISBN: 9781771589659
© On The Mark Press

Rose Fortune (1774-1864)
Slave, Entrepreneur, Policewoman

Rose Fortune was born into slavery in the British Colony in the state of Virginia. Her family was owned by the Devone family who were loyalists. During the American Revolution they travelled by ship with their slaves to relocate in Nova Scotia. After ten year old Rose and her family arrived in Annapolis Royal in Nova Scotia, the Devone family granted them their freedom.

Earning a living, in those days, was difficult for black loyalists who came to Canada but Rose Fortune was able to develop two good businesses in the area. Rose began by becoming a dock worker or 'baggage' carrier using a wheelbarrow. She would transport luggage and provisions from ships to hotels and homes. In 1841, Rose's business became known as the 'Lewis Transfer' and horse drawn wagons were used. Later Rose established a wake-up call service to alert people at nearby inns to be up in time to catch their ships leaving or for appointments that they had to attend. Her grandchildren carried on the Lewis Transfer business for the next 100 years.

Everyone living in Annapolis Royal knew who Rose was by her style of dress. Her appearance was unique and unforgetable. Rose would wear a dress with her petticoat hanging below its hem. Over her dress Rose wore an apron and a man's waistcoat. A lace cap was worn to cover her hair and a man's straw hat crowned her head. Rose wore men's boots that had heels to make her taller. Often she carried a basket. Her style of dressing was often worn by black pioneer women.

When Rose worked on the docks she discovered that teenage thugs were causing problems. She made herself the policewoman for the Port of Annapolis Royal. Teenagers that were caught were attacked and spanked by Rose. She also imposed and enforced curfews on the wharves and surrounding areas at Annapolis Royal harbour to protect visitors and tourists. Many people consider her the first policewoman in Canada.

Later Rose worked on the Underground Railroad and transported refugee slaves from the docks to safe houses. In 1884, Rose Fortune died at the age of 90.

SSR1135   ISBN: 9781771589659
© On The Mark Press

Rose Fortune (1174-1864)

Slave, Entrepreneur, Policewoman

A READING
Answer the questions.

1. Tell why you think it would be difficult for free black loyalists to get work in the 1800s in Nova Scotia.

_____

_____

2. What types of businesses were developed by Rose? _____

_____

_____

_____

3. Why was Rose easily recognized in Annapolis Royal? Describe her appearance. _____

_____

_____

4. Why did Rose make herself a policewoman and then looked after the docks? _____

_____

_____

5. How did Rose deal with the teenage thugs? _____

_____

6. Why did Rose establish and enforce curfews on the docks and the surrounding areas? _____

_____

7. How did Rose help refugee slaves? _____

_____

B LANGUAGE
The part of a sentence that names the person or thing is called the 'subject.' The part that tells what is said about the subject is called the 'predicate.' Underline the subject and circle the predicate in each sentence.

1. The ship sailed to the port full of loyalists.

2. Rose chased the foolish thugs away.

3. The wheelbarrow rolled down the street.

4. The man caught his ship on time

5. People stayed at nearby inns

6. Rose helped many slaves.

C WORD STUDY
Record the following groups of words in alphabetical order.

1. leaving, living, loyalists, luggage _____

2. curfew, consider, caught, carrier _____

3. worn, waistcoat, warn, wharves _____

4. transport, travelled, transfer, thugs _____

5. petticoat, problems, protect, provisions _____

SKILLS: Recalling Details | Subject/Predicate | Alphabetical Order

SSR1135 ISBN: 9781771589659
© On The Mark Press

Shawnadithit (1800-1829)
The Last of the Beothuk

A First Nation group called the Beothuk lived on the island of Newfoundland many years ago. They were tall, white-skinned people with black hair and black eyes. Then the Europeans arrived and changed their lifestyle. The Beothuk would be lured onto their ships and then carried off to be sold in slave markets in Europe This activity caused the Beothuks to not trust the 'buggishaman' as they called them and avoided them as they carried European guns.

The British settled in areas that were the Beothuks' main sources for food which were their best hunting and fishing grounds. The Beothuk began to die from starvation and the new diseases brought by the English settlers. After a period of time the Beothuk and the English began killing each other when the opportunity took place.

Around the year 1800, a baby girl called 'Shawnadithit' was born in a village near Red Indian Lake. While she was growing up Shawnadithit experienced seeing many tragedies take place. Her people were slowly dying from strange diseases or they were killed or captured for reward money. One day while washing some food in a stream, Shawnadithit was shot by a trapper and wounded in her hand and leg. She was able to crawl away and escape. One day she saw her aunt being captured and carried off by British men eager for reward money. Shawnadithit grew to be a young woman but she knew that she would never marry and have children because most of the young Beothuk men were dead.

In March of 1823, the few Beothuk who were alive were in need of food. Shawnadithit's uncle and cousin decided to travel to the sea coast to look for some. Shawnadithit stayed with her mother and sister, who were ill with tuberculosis at the village. Then her father decided to go out alone to hunt and when he didn't return they thought that he was dead. The three woman were so hungry they decided to walk to the sea coast themselves to find food. Along the way they stumbled across the bodies of Shawnadithit's uncle and cousin lying in the snow shot and killed by the 'buggishaman.' The women were so upset they hoped that they would be shot and killed and put out of their misery. They gave themselves up to a red-bearded trapper who they had seen murder other Beothuk. Instead of being killed the trapper forced them to march with him to the closest settlement so he could collect the reward money.

As they walked beside a frozen river suddenly they heard a voice shouting. It was Shawnadithit's father who was being chased by another British trapper. Shawnadithit's joy changed to horror as she saw the red-bearded trapper raise his musket. Her father was trapped between two armed buggishamen and he turned and ran across the ice-covered river. The ice broke and Shawnadithit watched as her father slowly sank beneath the swirling waters and drowned. The three women were taken to a British settlement where they were fed and cared for by the settlers. Later Shawnadithit's mother and sister died and she was alone. For five years she worked as an unpaid servant for a British family. During these years, Shawnadithit would often wander into the woods where she would talk and laugh with her sister and mother. These visits helped to keep her going. Many people in Newfoundland were upset with the disappearance of the Beothuk people. William Cormack, a Newfoundlander, decided to travel across the island and hoped to find and help any Beothuk people who were still alive. Unfortunately he could not find any. Then he heard about Shawnadithit and had her brought to St. John's in 1828. He believed that she was the last Beothuk alive and asked her to teach him about her people.

Shawnadithit was artistic and drew pictures of things her people used and maps for him of the island. She also taught him words in her language and about her people's customs and beliefs. While she told William Cormack about her people's last days she would weep. Unfortunately for Shawnadithit when she arrived in St. John's she had already contacted the same lung disease that killed her mother and sister. Ten months later at the age of 29 Shawnadithit died. This was a tragic end to a group of First Nation People.

Shawnadithit (1800-1829)

The Last of the Beothuk

A **READING**

Complete the following activities.

1. List the reasons why the Beothuk feared and mistrusted the Europeans. _____

_____

_____

2. List the reasons why the Beothuk population was shrinking in size. _____

_____

3. Tell why the Beothuk people were starving. _____

_____

4. What tragedies did Shawnadithit experience while growing up? _____

_____

_____

_____

5. How did the history of the Beothuk people get known? _____

_____

6. What information did Shawnadithit share with William Carmack? _____

_____

_____

7. Think of ways that this tragedy could have been prevented. _____

_____

_____

B **LANGUAGE**

Underline the subject and circle the predicate in each sentence.

1. The Beothuk lived on the island of Newfoundland.

2. The British settled along the coasts of the island.

3. The trapper shot the Beothuk woman.

4. The men captured her aunt.

5. Her father sank into the icy water.

C **WORD STUDY**

Divide the following words into syllables.

1. arrive _____

2. people _____

3. trapper _____

4. settlement _____

5. horror _____

6. starvation _____

7. swirling _____

8. settlers _____

9. disappearance _____

10. artistic _____

SSR1135   ISBN: 9781771589659
© On The Mark Press

Madeleine Jarret Tarieu (1678-1747)
Heroine of Verchères

During the years when Canada was first being settled by the French, the land was divided into land grants or 'seigneuries.' Each land owner was called a 'seigneur.' The land was then rented to families who paid their rent with small amounts of farm crops. The farm families were called 'habitants.'

François Jarret, a French soldier, was given a large seigneury on the St. Lawrence River for his service to France. Jarret called the seigneury Verchères. François and his wife Marie Perrot had twelve children and their fourth child, Madeleine became known as the courageous Madeleine of Verchères.

This area in new France was rich in animal life, fish, birds, wood, and wild fruits. Madeleine's father taught all of his children how to load and shoot a musket properly. Madeleine was an excellent shot and often went hunting with her family.

In 1681, the Iroquois were no longer at peace with the French settlers. They felt they were being cut off from the fur trade by the French. The English, who were their allies and trading partners, encouraged them to attack the French. François Jarret's first duty as a seigneur was to protect his family and the habitants. He had a fort built with wooden walls five metres high in a rectangular shape around his family home and the other buildings and called it 'Fort Verchères.' It was also known as 'Dangerous Castle.' If the Iroquois ever attacked the fort it would take one day for soldiers to come from the French settlement of Montreal.

On October of 1692, a large group of Iroquois attacked Fort Verchères and quickly captured many habitants who were working in the fields outside the fort. Fourteen year old Madeleine Jarret was also working outside in a vegetable garden that was close to the gate of Fort Verchères. When she saw an Iroquois warrior quickly approaching her, Madeleine rushed through the gate, slammed it shut and gave the alarm "Too Arms! Too Arms!" she shouted loudly.

There were mainly women and children in the fort and they were depending on her to be their leader. Madeleine quickly climbed onto the stockades wearing a soldier's hat and stood with her brothers and the only soldier in the fort. She shouted and gave orders as if the fort was full of soldiers so the Iroquois would think it would be too hard to attack and destroy.

Madeleine fired off a small canon as a warning to the other French forts along the St. Lawrence River and to signal for help. She knew that the other forts would pass along the message to the Montreal soldiers that Fort Verchères was under attack. The Iroquois had completely surrounded the fort. Madeleine knew it would take the soldiers a full day to get there. She waited and watched and did not dare to eat or sleep as she knew the Iroquois preferred making surprise attacks. Madeleine would not even let in the lowing cattle standing at the gate for fear Iroquois might be hiding under cattle skins and would get into the fort.

Sometime the next day the Iroquois disappeared into the forest and an hour later help had arrived from Montreal. One hundred French soldiers came by boat and fifty native allies came by land. The native allies who may have been the Algonquin or Montagnais caught up with the Iroquois war party on Lake Champlain and freed the captured French settlers and brought them back to Fort Verchères. Madeleine de Verchères was a woman of valour and determination!

SSR1135   ISBN: 9781771589659
© On The Mark Press

Madeleine Jarret Tarieu (1678-1747)
Heroine of Verchères

A READING
Complete the following activities.

1. List five other possible dangers early settlers might have experienced while settling in Canada.

_____

_____

_____

2. In what ways did Madeleine act like a heroine?

_____

_____

_____

3. Record the following sentences in the correct order to form a paragraph describing Madeleine's adventure.

   • Donning a soldier's cap, Madeleine climbed up onto the stockade beside her brothers and the one soldier and prepared to shoot.

   • One day while working in a garden outside the fort, Madeleine saw an Iroquois approaching her.

   • When the others began shooting at the Iroquois, Madeleine fired off a canon to tell other forts that they needed help.

   • The next day help arrived and the prisoners held by the Iroquois were freed, the Iroquois had disappeared, and the fort was saved.

   • She quickly ran into the fort, closed the gate, and began shouting orders.

_____

_____

_____

_____

_____

_____

_____

B LANGUAGE
A modifier is often a group of words called a *word-group modifier*. In the sentences below, underline the word-group modifier. Example: Pupils study <u>in this room</u>.

1. Groups of Iroquois were approaching the fort.

2. The Iroquois moved about carefully and quietly

3. Madeleine knew how to use a gun properly.

4. The next day the Iroquois disappeared into the forest.

5. One hundred soldiers came by boat.

C WORD STUDY
Complete each word with the correct vowel combination: ai   ou   au   ea   oo   ui   ou

1. p _____ d	2. am _____ nts	3. t _____ ght	4. p _____ ce	5. w _____ den
6. sh _____ ted	7. m _____ nly	8. l _____ der	9. st _____ d	10. w _____ ted
11. f _____ r	12. ar _____ nd	13. y _____ rs	14. fr _____ ts	15. gr _____ p

SSR1135   ISBN: 9781771589659
© On The Mark Press

Silken Laumann
A Determined Sculler

1. Silken Laumann is the greatest female rower ever to come out of Canada. She was born on November 14 in 1964 in Mississauga, Ontario. Silken began her athletic career as a runner at the age of 17 and then turned to rowing along with her sister Danièle. The Laumann sisters quickly advanced to the Canadian National Team and in 1984 at Los Angeles, California they won a bronze medal in the Olympic double sculls.

2. When Danièle retired Silken took on different partners and also began to scull as a single as well. After a disappointing 7th place finish in the double sculls event in the 1988 Olympic Games in Seoul, South Korea, Silken moved to the single scull and trained with the men's team. In 1991, she became the best women's rower in the world and won the World Cup Championship and the World Championship in sculling that year.

3. In 1992, many people felt that Silken was the favourite sculler who would capture the gold medal at the Barcelona Summer Olympics in Spain. One day, in Lessen Germany, while Silken was training on a lake an unfortunate accident took place. Her scull and the scull of a German team collided injuring one of Silken's legs. When Silken looked down at her leg she knew immediately that it was a serious injury as she could see her leg muscle hanging beside her ankle and the bone of her leg was exposed. Silken was rushed to a local hospital where she had to endure five operations on her leg and had to rest there for three weeks. By late June, this amazing athlete was back on the water training again. When Silken sat in her scull for the first time after her accident she was so happy that she began to cry. She realized then just how much she loved her sport as the doctors had forecast that she may never be able to row again.

4. Silken's gold medal win may have been doomed but she refused to give up. At the Barcelona Olympics, Silken did not win gold but her bronze medal shone as brightly as a gold one. She was named Canadian of the Year by the Canadian Club and was selected to carry the Canadian Flag in the Closing Ceremonies of the Barcelona Olympics. After the Olympics, Silken took a year off training to allow her leg to heal properly.

5. In 1994, Silken began competing again. She won a silver medal at the 1995 World Championships. During the same year, Silken won a gold medal as part of a scull team at the Pan American Games. Her final competitive race was at the 1996 Summer Olympics in Atlanta, Georgia where she won a silver medal in single sculls. In 1999, Silken Laumann announced that she was retiring from the sport. In 1998, Silken was inducted into the Sports Hall of Fame and was also awarded the Thomas Keller Medal in 1999 for her outstanding international rowing career.

Silken's courageous performance at the Barcelona Olympics in 1992 will never be forgotten.

SSR1135 ISBN: 9781771589659
© On The Mark Press

Silken Lauman
A Determined Sculler

A READING
Complete the following activity.

1. Match the information sentence to its numbered paragraph in the story.

_____ Silken Lauman's change in sporting events was successful.

_____ Silken and Danièle were sisters and successful scullers.

_____ Silken experienced a tragic accident while training.

_____ Silken Lauman was a fighter and was determined to participate.

_____ Silken was honoured with special awards.

_____ Everyone felt that Silken would win the gold medal at the Olympics.

2. Brainstorm for words that describe Silken Lauman as a person and an athlete.

_____

_____

_____

_____

B LANGUAGE
Underline the nouns and circle the pronouns in each sentence.

1. They won a bronze medal in double sculls.

2. When Silken looked at it she knew her leg was badly injured.

3. While she was in the hospital the doctors performed five operations on it.

4. In Atlanta, Silken won a silver medal in single sculls.

C WORD STUDY
Locate the verb in the story that matches each of the following meanings.

1. went forward	_____	6. suffer	_____
2. to stop working	_____	7. ended	_____
3. to catch or win	_____	8. gleamed	_____
4. crashed together	_____	9. picked	_____
5. could be seen	_____	10. practised	_____

SSR1135   ISBN: 9781771589659
© On The Mark Press

Hayley Wickenheiser
One of Canada's Finest Athletes

Hayley Wickenheiser is considered the greatest female hockey player in the world. In 2003, Hayley was the first female player to score a point in a men's professional game when she played in the Finnish hockey league. Hayley was named the MVP of Canada's gold medal-winning team at both the 2002 Salt Lake City and 2006 Torino Winter Olympics. Her talent is unsurpassed. Hayley has won the most gold medals of any Canadian Olympian. She has represented Canada five times at the Winter Olympics and has captured four gold and one silver medal.

Hayley Wickenheiser was born on August 12, in 1978, in Shaunavon, Saskatchewan and is the oldest of three children. She learned to skate on a backyard rink created by her parents at the age of six. On this rink is where Hayley's love for hockey began. As a youngster, she played on a local boys' team and was the only girl. On many occasions, Hayley had to put on her hockey gear in boiler rooms and other places in rinks as there were seldom any available dressing rooms. It was a fight for her to be enrolled in a hockey school in Swift Current, where again she was the only girl. Finally, her family moved to Calgary, Alberta so she could play on an all-girls' team in the city. In 1991, Hayley was a member of Team Alberta and played in the Under-17 Girls' Competition at the Canada Winter Games. During the competition, Hayley helped her team win a gold medal by scoring the winning goal and was named MVP of the final game.

In 1994, at the age of 15, Hayley was chosen to play on Canada's National Women's Team. Her teammates who were much older than her nicknamed her 'Highchair Hayley' because she was so young. At her first international tournament, at the 1994 World Championships held in Lake Placid, her team won gold. In 1997, at her second World Championship, her team captured the gold and Hayley earned a spot on the tournament All-Star Team which was the first of four times for her to be chosen. In 1999, Hayley helped Canada to win another gold medal and became the tournament MVP. Hayley has six World Championship gold medals and two silver medals.

Hayley was a member of Team Canada at the 1998 Winter Olympics which was the first time women's hockey was introduced as a sport. Canada won a silver medal and Hayley was named to the tournament all-star team. In 2002, Hayley made the roster again for Team Canada and played in the Winter Olympics held in Salt Lake City, Utah. This time Canada beat the United States in the final game for the gold medal. During the 2006 Winter Olympics in Torino, Italy, Canada was defending its gold medal status. Team Canada played against Sweden, a surprise finalist, and won gold. This time Hayley was awarded MVP, Top Forward, and a place on the all-star team. In 2010, in Vancouver, Canada's hockey team won the gold medal and in 2014 at the Sochi Olympics they repeated winning the gold. At the Sochi Olympics, Hayley was elected to the International Olympic Committee or IOC by the athletes.

During her hockey career, Hayley continued her studies at the University of Calgary in its pre-med program. In 2000, she qualified for a spot on the Canadian women's softball team and travelled to the 2000 Summer Olympics in Sydney, Australia. She is the second Canadian woman to ever compete in both the Winter and Summer Olympics.

Hayley is considered by many to be the greatest female ice hockey player in the world.

SSR1135 ISBN: 9781771589659
© On The Mark Press

Image credit: Iurii Osadchi / Shutterstock.com

Hayley Wickenheiser
One of Canada's Finest Athletes

A READING
Complete the following activities.

1. What difficulties did young girls experience years ago if they wanted to play hockey?

_____

_____

_____

2. Do girls have the same problems today? Explain your answer.

_____

_____

3. List reasons why Hayley Wickenheiser is an outstanding Canadian athlete.

_____

_____

_____

4. Explain why you think Hayley is a suitable role model for young girls who wish to play hockey.

_____

_____

_____

5. In order to become a hockey player like Hayley, what skills and type of personality should a girl have?

_____

_____

_____

B LANGUAGE
Record the correct tense for the following verbs. Is it *present*, *past*, or *future*?

1. learned _____
2. score _____
3. captured _____
4. will enroll _____
5. win _____

6. will move _____
7. helped _____
8. fought _____
9. won _____
10. fighting _____

C WORD STUDY
Record the word *singular*, *plural*, or *possessive* after each of the following nouns.

1. games _____
2. Hayley's _____
3. teams _____
4. medal _____
5. parents _____

6. medals _____
7. boys' _____
8. women's _____
9. times _____
10. competition _____

SKILLS: Fact and Opinion | Kinds of Nouns | Verb Tenses

SSR1135   ISBN: 9781771589659
© On The Mark Press

Joannie Rochette
The Performance of a Lifetime

Joannie Rochette was born in Montreal, Québec and was raised in a small community called Île Dupas. She was the only child of Therese and Normand Rochette. One day, at the age of two, Joannie watched some people skating on the St. Lawrence River near her home. She asked her father if she could do it too and he helped her put on some skates. As Joannie grew up she often skated on the river while her parents were ice fishing.

Joannie began formal ice skating training at a local arena. Her mother was her number one fan and took her back and forth to the rink and often stayed to watch her daughter. Joannie's mother pushed her to do well in whatever she did, including school and ice skating. They had a very close relationship and her mother supported her whole-heartedly. Joannie's father worked tirelessly to support his family and her ice skating. Ice skating training and equipment is very expensive. Many times the local community held fund raising dinners to help pay for her skating bills.

When Joannie was thirteen years old she moved to Trois Rivières to train with coach Manon Perron. This meant that the only time Joannie would see her parents was on the weekend. Leaving home to return to Trois Rivières brought many tears. As Joannie matured and her skating skills were well developed, she competed in many important ice skating competitions and won various gold, silver, and bronze medals.

Joannie Rochette is a six-time Canadian National Champion. She won silver at the 2009 World Ice Skating Championships; silver at 2008 and 2009 Four Continent Championships; and bronze at the 2004 Grand Prix Final.

At the 2010 Winter Olympics in Vancouver, Joannie Rochette had to face the music alone. Two days before she was to compete in the Ladies Short Program, Joannie received the devastating news that her mother had died of a heart attack after arriving in Vancouver to watch her skate. Many wondered how she would have the strength and energy to perform.

With the support of her fellow skaters, skating coaches, her wonderful father, and the audience in the Pacific Coliseum, and all the people in Canada, Joannie bravely skated alone on the vast white ice surface and carved out two memorable programs in the alloted time. During both of her programs the audience held their breath hoping and wanting to see her do well. After each performance the audience loudly cheered and applauded.

Joannie achieved excellent results under immense, emotional strain that few people in the world would be able to understand. She finished her last program with a kiss to the sky and the words "This one was for you!" She had won the bronze medal.

What a brave young athlete!

SSR1135   ISBN: 9781771589659
© On The Mark Press
   Image credit: Olga Besnard / Shutterstock.com

Joannie Rochette
The Performance of a Lifetime

A
Complete the following activities.

1. Joannie Rochette and her mother had a very strong relationship. Think of ways that such a strong relationship could develop between a child and a parent.

_____

_____

_____

2. If your community had a talented athlete involved in ice skating or another sport, what are some of the ways it could help? List the ways.

_____

_____

_____

3. Think of reasons why competing at the 2010 Winter Olympics was so difficult for Joannie?

_____

_____

_____

4. Circle the words in each row that best describe Joannie's personality during the 2010 Winter Olympics.

weak	scared	strong	selfish	brave	stoic	cold
naughty	silly	outstanding	controlled	good	terrible	poor
honourable	emotional	committed	horrible	loyal	thankful	sad

B LANGUAGE
Is the underlined verb in each sentence in the *present*, *past*, or *future* tense. Record the tense on the line.

1. Joannie Rochette <u>trained</u> with coach Manon Perron.   _____

2. Joannie <u>hopes</u> to skate well for her mother.   _____

3. Joannie <u>will skate</u> in the show called 'Stars on Ice.'   _____

4. She often <u>skated</u> on the St. Lawrence River in the winter.   _____

5. Joannie <u>will remember</u> the days she spent with her mother often.   _____

C WORD STUDY
Skim through the story to find antonyms for the following words.

1. large   _____

2. never   _____

3. far   _____

4. lost   _____

5. poor   _____

6. many   _____

7. began   _____

8. returning   _____

9. together   _____

10. cheap   _____

 SKILLS: Giving an Opionion | Classifying | Verb Tenses | Antonyms   SSR1135 ISBN: 9781771589659   © On The Mark Press

Jennifer Jones
Canada's Curling Star

One of Canada's greatest curlers was born on July 7, 1974 in Winnipeg, Manitoba. As a very young child she fell in love with curling while watching her parents play games at their curling club. Jennifer was very athletic as a child growing up and played many different sports but never found one that she really liked. When she was eleven, Jennifer's parents introduced her to curling. Being an only child, her parents were always there to help her. As a student at school Jennifer loved to solve problems and to develop strategies to figure them out. Using strategy is an important skill in the game of curling.

During her early curling career, Jennifer played in three provincial and national junior competitions. At the age of 16, Jennifer and her team won their first provincial junior title. After winning the junior championship, Jennifer wanted to get better and become more well-known. One of her big dreams was to play at the Scotties Tournament and to win. Jennifer did get her opportunity to curl at it. In her final game, final end, and her last rock, Jennifer had a difficult shot to make and the pressure was tremendous. This shot was perfectly completed and her team won the Scotties Tournament and this also gave her a spot at the World Curling Championships.

The World Curling Championships were a major disappointment for Jennifer and her team as they were knocked out of the playoffs. Fortunately Jennifer is a curler who is able to get over a loss and pick herself and her team back up quickly. Jennifer and her team competed regularly at the Scotties hoping to accomplish something more.

Finally their chance came at the 2013 Olympic Trials where the team won the right to represent Canada as the Canadian Womens' Curling Team at the 2014 Sochi Olympics. At the Olympics, Jennifer Jones, Kaitlyn Lowes, Jill Officer, and Dawn McEwan won every single frame in the round robin giving themselves a clear pathway to the finals. Team Canada won the finals and the gold medal. All of their hard work had not been in vain.

Canada is proud of its Curling Queen and her three princesses!

SSR1135 ISBN: 9781771589659
© On The Mark Press

Image credit: Jamie Roach / Shutterstock.com

Jennifer Jones
Canada's Curling Star

A READING

Record the first five words of each sentence in the story that describes...

1. when Jennifer Jones began to curl

_____

2. an important curling skill

_____

3. when Jennifer Jones won her first provincial junior title

_____

4. how Jennifer won her first Scotties Tournament

_____

5. how Jennifer and her team got the opportunity to go to the Olympics.

_____

6. how well Jennifer and her team played at the Olympic round robin.

_____

7. what the Jones team won at the 2014 Sochi Olympics.

_____

8. Jennifer's dream

_____

B LANGUAGE

A *phrase* is a group of words that begins with a *preposition*. It describes how something looks or how something moves. Underline the phrases in each sentence below.

1. Jennifer loved to solve problems at school.

2. She liked to watch her parents curl on the ice.

3. At the 2013 Olympic Trials, her team won the right to represent Canada at the 2014 Sochi Olympics.

4. After a loss, Jennifer is able to quickly get back to competing again.

C WORD STUDY

Locate the words in the story that have the following meanings.

1. occupation, job _____   5. famous, important _____

2. hard, not easy _____   6. horrible, frightful _____

3. most important _____   7. a good chance _____

4. to try hard to win _____   8. a contest of athletes _____

SSR1135   ISBN: 9781771589659
© On The Mark Press

Kaillie Humphries
Bobsledding Olympian

Kaillie Humphries is a Canadian bobsledder. She was born on September 4, 1985 in Calgary, Alberta. Humphries and her partner, Heather Moyse, from Summerside, P.E.I. were Olympic Champions in bobsledding in the 2010 Winter Olympics. They were also the first Canadian women to pilot a Canadian bobsled team to victory at an Olympics. Humphries was also the first female driver to win the World Championship in a bobsled competition.

Kaillie began her athletic career at the age of 16 as an alpine ski racer. She always dreamed of winning an Olympic gold medal in the sport but realized it would be very difficult to get chosen for the national team. Kaillie then turned to the bobsled. During her first four years she was a bobsled brakeman and was named as an alternate to the Canadian team at the 2006 Olympic Winter Games. Because Kaillie did not get a chance to compete in Torino she thought of trying out for the British team as she was planning to marry Don Humphries, a brakeman on the British team in 2006 and then she could apply for British Citizenship. Fortunately for Canada and Bobsled Canada, Kaillie changed her mind and remained in the Canadian program.

Read the following facts to find out how Kaillie Humphries' career grew.

- **2006-2007**: Kaillie progressed from a rookie bobsled pilot to an elite bobsled driver. At the Europa Cup she won 3 events as a pilot and topped the overall standings. At the 2007 Junior World Bobsled Championships in Germany, Kaillie won a silver medal with her partner.

- **2007-2008**: Kaillie and her partner Shelly-Ann Brown of Pickering, Ontario captured a bronze medal at a competition in Lake Placid, New York.

- **2008-2009**: Kaillie had two more silver podium finishes with her partner Sally-Ann Brown and a World Cup silver with Heather Moyse at a World Cup competition in Whistler, B.C. Their success at the Whistler World Cup made them serious medal contenders at the 2010 Olympic Games in Vancouver. Two months before the Olympics, Humphries and Moyse won two silver medals and one bronze medal at european competitions.

- **2010**: At the Vancouver Winter Olympics, Humphries and Moyse set records in their start and finishing times and won the gold medal.

- **2011**: Humphries and Brown won the bronze medal at the World Bobsled Championships.

- **2012**: Humphries with a new partner won her first World Championship at Lake Placid, New York. She became the first female Canadian bobsled driver to win that title.

- **2013**: This was one of Humphries best seasons. She won six of nine World Cup races and the World Bobsled Championships. Humphries and Moyse reunited and won the World Cup event of the season at Calgary's Olympic Park. Their start time of 5.45 seconds was a record.

- **2014**: Humphries and Moyse battled against their American rivals and won their consecutive gold medal by the tenth of a second at the Sochi Winter Olympics.

Kaillie Humphries' persistence and determination made her dream come true.

SSR1135   ISBN: 9781771589659
© On The Mark Press

Image credit: Iurii Osadchi / Shutterstock.com

Kaillie Humphries

Bobsledding Olympian

A READING

Record the year(s) that each of the following events took place in Kaillie's career.

1. Kaillie and her partner won a bronze medal in a competition in Lake Placid, New York. _____

2. Humphries and Moyse, set start and finishing times and won the gold medal. _____

3. Humphries became an official bobsled pilot. _____

4. Humphries and Moyse won a silver medal at a World Cup in Whistler, British Columbia. _____

5. Humphries and a new partner won their first World Championship at Lake Placid. _____

6. Humphries and Moyse won two silver medals and one bronze medal at european competitions.

   _____

7. At a Junior World Bobsledding Championship, Kaillie and her partner won a silver medal. _____

8. Humphries and Moyse reunited and won the World Cup event at Calgary's Olympic Park. _____

B LANGUAGE

Underline the *adjective phrase* and circle the *adverb phrase* in each sentence.

1. Kaillie loved sliding swiftly down the track.

2. The brakeman of a bobsled team must quickly push the sled down the course.

3. The pilot of a team steers the bobsled down the icy course.

4. They were one of the fastest teams in the last run.

5. In the closing ceremonies Kaillie and Heather were delighted to carry Canada's flag.

C WORD STUDY

Locate words in the story that match each meaning and syllable count.

1. a large athletic contest; 4 syllables _____

2. to be lucky; 4 syllables _____

3. one of the best; 2 syllables _____

4. joined together again; 4 syllables _____

5. to drive or steer; 2 syllables _____

6. not easy; 3 syllables _____

7. beginner; 2 syllables _____

8. fought; 2 syllables _____

SSR1135   ISBN: 9781771589659
© On The Mark Press

Tessa Virtue and Scott Moir
The King and Queen of Ice Dancing

Tessa Virtue and Scott Moir have been dancing together for 17 years and were both born in London, Ontario but Scott was raised in Ilderton. They both skated at the same club but became more familiar with each other at the summer skate camps held at the Ilderton arena. Scott's aunt, Carol Moir had coached him with another partner and when she decided to give up skating, his aunt noticed that Tessa was the right size and her skill level in dance matched Scott's. Their partnership began and they began competing in 1998.

Eventually Tessa and Scott required additional training and their coach Carol Moir, sought out Paul MacIntosh, a prominent coach in Kitchener to teach them one day a week. After winning the provincial finals in January of 1999, they knew they needed to increase their training time and moved to Waterloo permanently. For the next few years, Tessa and Scott travelled at home and abroad. As junior ice dance skaters they competed in Skate Slovakia, Tomorrow's Champions, the North American Challenge, and the Croatia Cup. When they won first place at the Junior Nationals in Edmonton in 2004, Tessa and Scott travelled to the Junior Worlds in the Hague and again took first place. This success at the junior level of dancing made them seek better training and they sought out Zoveve and Igor Shpitband in Clinton, Michigan at their training centre. Tessa and Scott competed at the Junior Level internationally in 2004 and 2005 but competed as seniors in Canadian Competitions. They had hoped to compete at the 2006 Winter Olympics but were passed over. This made them very determined to compete at the Vancouver 2010 Winter Olympics.

In the summer of 2007, Tessa began to feel cramps and pains in her shins but continued to train and they finished second at the NHK Competition and the World Competition, and first place at the Canadian Championships. The pain continued and finally she was diagnosed to have chronic exertional compartment syndrome. In October of 2008 Tessa had surgery on both shins and while Tessa was recovering, Scott continued to train by himself. During 2009, Tessa and Scott began training again in short sessions as Tessa was still experiencing pain. Despite the setback, they came first at 2009 Canadian Nationals and the Trophee Eric Bomard, second at the Four Continents, and third at the World Championships.

In 2010 Virtue and Moir won the Canadian Nationals which prepared them for the 2010 Winter Olympics in Vancouver. Tessa and Scott wanted very much to impress the home crowd in the Pacific Coliseum during their compulsory and free dance programs. Two days before their compulsory dance program, Tessa experienced pain in her legs. They could not complete a full run through all of their routines. Despite the setback Virtue and Moir placed second in the compulsory dance and first in the original dance and were sitting in first place in that part of their competition. On February 22, 2010, Tessa and Scott were ready to impress and dazzle the home crowd. All eyes of the audience were focused on them as they danced back and forth over the ice and completed the challenging lift the pair had developed and called 'The Goose.' They were awarded a score of 110.42 points along with four perfect tens. It was the highest score of their career. Tessa and Scott became the First North Americans to win the Olympic gold medal in ice dance. During the same year they finished in first place at the World Championships.

Virtue and Moir kept on competing and faced their rivals Davis and White at many competitions battling for first place. During the two years before the 2014 Olympics, it was quite evident that something was happening to each pairs' dance scores. Davis and White were often rated higher in certain elements than Virtue and Moir. It appeared that one of the judges was fiddling with the marks which is not uncommon in ice skating. When the Sochi Olympic Games took place in 2014, Davis and White won the gold medal and Virtue and Moir the silver.

In the eyes of Canadians, Virtue and Moir will always be the golden ones who made ice dancing look spectacular, graceful, fast flowing, and very entertaining!

SSR1135   ISBN: 9781771589659
© On The Mark Press

Image credit: Olga Besnard / Shutterstock.com

Tessa Virtue and Scott Moir
The King and Queen of Ice Dancing

A READING
Complete the following activities.

1. Tessa and Scott have similar personality traits that have made them a very successful skating team. Circle the words below that could be used to decribe their personalities.

understanding	nasty	lackadaisical	critical	patient	committed
negative	honourable	selfish	negative	ambitious	jealous
friendship	easily discouraged	passionate	hard-working	fearful	frustrated
agreeable	aggressive	competitive	disinterested	impatient	envious

2. Although having the same personality traits is important in an ice dancing team so are physical similarities. Underline the words below that describe their physical similarities.

strong dance skills	good coordination	poor timing	no rhythm	athletic
clumsy	no feelings shown	good balance	awkward	soft knees
expressive	weak	flexible	rhythmical	similar bodies
fearsome	natural aptitude	physically strong	good posture	tense

3. Describe Virtue and Moir's performances at the 2014 Olympics and where they placed.

_____

_____

_____

_____

4. Do you think the methods used to judge ice dancing are fair, or should they be changed?

_____

_____

_____

B LANGUAGE
On the line at the end of each sentence, record the part of speech underlined.

1. Tessa and Scott danced <u>gracefully</u> across the ice. _____

2. Scott's aunt <u>coached</u> the dance pair at first. _____

3. Tessa began to feel <u>cramps</u> and <u>pains</u> in her shins. _____

4. The <u>huge</u> audience stood up and clapped after Tessa and Scott skated. _____

C WORD STUDY
Record the root word for each of the following words.

1. youngest _____

2. skating _____

3. provincial _____

4. competition _____

5. medallist _____

6. fiddling _____

7. battling _____

8. winning _____

 SKILLS: Classifying Vocabulary | Expressing Ideas/Opinions
| Parts of Speech | Root Words

SSR1135   ISBN: 9781771589659
© On The Mark Press

Eric Lamaze
Canada's Top Equestrian Rider

Eric Lamaze was born on April 17 in 1968 in Montreal, Québec. While growing up he did not have a father, that he knew, and his mother was in prison for drug trafficing so he was cared for and raised by his grandmother who was an alcoholic. While growing up he was taught to ride horses by a well known coach in Montreal by the name of Diane Dubic at a stable called Day by Day. Dubic helped Lamaze to get through his unstable childhood and helped him to turn his life around. At the age of 15, Eric dropped out of school to work for other equestran riders. He would do work for them and in exchange they gave him opportunities to ride their horses. This helped Eric to change his immature riding abilities into pure talent.

During the 1990's, Eric's career took off and he began competing at the Grand Prix (top-level) Competition in 1992 and a year later he was named to the Canadian Equestrian Team. In 1994, Eric represented Canada at the World Equestrian Games and finished in second place in the Canadian World Cup League standings. Although Eric continued to excel in the show ring, his success and reputation began to stumble. At the 1996 Olympic Games at Atlanta, Georgia, Lamaze tested positive for drug use (cocaine) and was banned from equestrian riding for four years. During an appeal, his suspension was then reduced to seven months.

In the year 2000, Lamaze earned a spot on the Canadian Olympic team but was again removed from the team because he tested positive for banned substances such as cold medication, diet pills, and later cocaine. This time the ban was for life but it was also overturned. For the next seven years, Lamaze spent time building his damaged career. While rebuilding his career he built his Torey Pines Stable in Schomberg, Ontario into a successful enterprise by trading horses and training riders. He also continued to perform for Canada in World Equestrian Championships in 1998, 2002, and 2006.

In 2007, Lamaze won Canada's richest show jumping purse of one million dollars at the One Million CN International Competition at Spruce Meadows in Alberta. He was also ranked in the top ten in the world and became the first rider to win prize money in the excess of one million dollars in a year. For Lamaze's efforts he was named 'Equine Canada's Equestrian of the Year.'

In 2008, Lamaze secured a spot on the Canadian Olympic Team heading for the Bejing Olympics. At this event, Eric's ride on Hickstead helped Canada's team win the silver medal. Later in the same games, Lamaze and Hickstead won an individual medal in a jump-off against a Swedish rider. It was Canada's first gold medal in the sport.

Eric Lamaze and Hickstead's relationship was very strong. Hickstead was a fiesty stallion who loved to hear the applause and cheers of audiences as they flew over the jumps. Unfortunately, during a competition in Verona, Italy in November of 2011, Hickstead collapsed shortly after finishing a round and died of an aortic rupture. This tragedy was witnessed by many people and shocked the riding community. Lamaze was devastated and misses Hickstead but life must go on. Eric continues to ride other horses at various competitions around the world.

Eric Lamaze and Hickstead were partners in a sport but also in Eric's hopes and ambitions. There is an old equestrian saying: 'For every rider there is one horse and for every horse there is one rider.'

SSR1135 ISBN: 9781771589659
© On The Mark Press

Image credit: catwalker / Shutterstock.com

Eric Lamaze
Canada's Top Equestrian Rider

A READING
Complete the following activities.

1. Do you think Eric's childhood experiences affected him later on in his life? Tell why or why not.

_____

_____

_____

2. Why do you think Eric used drugs during his career?

_____

_____

3. In what ways did Hickstead help Eric to achieve his goals during his career?

_____

_____

4. Lamaze was ranked in the top ten equestrian riders after winning at what big event?

_____

5. At what event did Lamaze and Hickstead win a gold and silver medal?

_____

6. What tragedy did Eric Lamaze have to overcome in 2011?

_____

B LANGUAGE
Record the name of the part(s) of speech that has been underlined in each sentence.

1. Eric <u>dropped</u> out <u>of school</u> when <u>he</u> was <u>fifteen</u>.

_____

2. <u>Lamaze</u> <u>secured</u> a <u>spot</u> <u>on the Canadian Olympic Team</u>.

_____

3. <u>Hickstead</u> and <u>Lamaze</u> <u>approached</u> the <u>jump</u>, <u>rose</u> high <u>into the air</u> <u>in</u> order to clear it.

_____

C WORD STUDY
Locate the words in the story that are antonyms to the words below.

1. negative _____	2. poorest _____	3. leaving _____
4. earlier _____	5. stopped _____	6. strong _____

Locate the words in the story that are synonyms to the words below.

1. chances _____	2. prevented _____	3. fell down _____
4. surprised _____	5. ability _____	6. young _____

SKILLS: Recalling Details |Opinions | Parts of Speech | Antonyms/Synonyms   SSR1135   ISBN: 9781771589659
© On The Mark Press

Alexandre Despatie
A Diver With Passion

Alexandre Despatie is a famous Canadian diver on the one and three metre springboards. He was born in Montreal, Québec on June 8, 1985. At the age of five he displayed the talent of becoming a diver in his family's pool. His talent in this sport was strongly supported by his mother, father, and sister. Read the following interesting facts about Alex's sport and career:

- World Champion of the one and three metre springboards from 2005 to 2007

- First and so far the only diver to have been a world champion in three categories – the 1, 3, and 10 metre platform diving.

- Alex is also a 37 time Canadian senior diving champion and 9 time junior champion.

- At the age of 13 he gained public attention at the 1998 Commonwealth Games by winning the gold medal with scores of perfect 10's. This achievement was recorded in the Guinness Book of World Records in the year 2000.

- At the 2000 Olympic Games in Sydney, Australia, Alex began his storybook diving career by placing fourth on the 10 metre platform.

- Before or at each of Despatie's three previous Olympics he had to overcome severe challenges and injuries. Before the Sydney Olympics in Australia, at the age of 14, Alex missed diving for three months with an ailing back injury. At the Athens, Olympics, Alex was defending his 10 metre World Championships platform diving record but his poor performance did not give him a medal. On the springboard Despatie did win the silver medal but his poor performances overall made him think it is time to retire.

- During the Beijing Olympics, Despatie competed on a barely healed foot that he had in a cast just months before the games. At these games, he was able to capture a silver medal in the 3 metre springboard and placed fifth in the 3 metre synchro.

- It was a miracle that Alex was able to compete in the London Olympic Games in England. The many competitions and training periods had left him with a broken body. A team of athletic therapists reconstructed his body and mind to total fitness that carried him through the London Olympic Games and into his planned acting career.

- An unfortunate accident took place in a Grand Prix meet in Madrid, Spain. While practising an inward 3 1/2 somersault, that Alex could do in his sleep, he slammed his head on the diving board splitting open his forehead at the hairline so badly that he required surgery.

- At his forth and final Olympics in London, England in 2012 at the age of 27 Alex finished his career in an unaccustomed spot in the 3 metre springboard final. He placed 11th or second from the last. Although Alex Despatie did not achieve the results he hoped for he felt that he had done his best and did everything he needed to do to be at the games.

- Despatie revolutionized the art of diving in Canada and changed attitudes of many towards the sport. He is an amazing athlete that responded and came back from many injuries to participate in the sport he so loved and brought great honour to Canada.

What an outstanding Canadian athlete!

SSR1135   ISBN: 9781771589659
© On The Mark Press

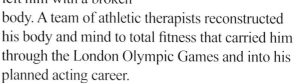

Image credit: Mitch Gunn / Shutterstock.com

Alexandre Despatie
A Diver With Passion

A **READING**

Record on the line when each event took place in Alex's diving career.

1. Placed fourth on the 10 metre platform which began his diving career.

_____

2. Had scores of perfect 10's at the age of 13.

_____

3. World Champion on the 1 metre and 3 metre springboard.

_____

4. Alex missed diving for three months because of a back injury.

_____

5. Competed after his heel had barely healed but captured a silver medal in the 3 metre spring board.

_____

6. A team of athletic therapists put his body and mind together so he could compete at this competition.

_____

7. During a practise session at this competition Alex banged his head on the spring board splitting it open.

_____

8. Alex completed his diving career at the age of 27 even though he did not win a medal.

_____

B **LANGUAGE**

Identify each underlined word's part of speech. Record the names on the line in order.

1. When <u>Alex</u> was fourteen <u>he</u> <u>received</u> <u>perfect</u> scores in diving.

_____

2. His <u>poor</u> <u>performances</u> did not <u>give</u> <u>him</u> a medal in the competition.

_____

3. The <u>many</u> <u>competitions</u> and <u>training</u> <u>periods</u> <u>left</u> Alex <u>with</u> a <u>broken</u> body.

_____

4. During practice <u>in</u> <u>Spain</u> Alex <u>slammed</u> his <u>head</u> on the <u>diving</u> board.

_____

C **WORD STUDY**

Record the vowel sounds that you can hear in each word on the line beside each one.
Example: public – short u, short i

1. platform _____

2. severe _____

3. retire _____

4. springboard _____

5. achieve _____

6. athletic _____

SSR1135   ISBN: 9781771589659
© On The Mark Press

Steve Nash
A Basketball Wonder

Who would have thought that a skinny Canadian kid would want to play the game of basketball in the major leagues. In his youth, Nash had to beg college coaches to just take a look at him. Today he has the basketball world at his feet.

Steve Nash was born in Johannesburg, South Africa on February 7, 1974. His father was a professional soccer player and the family moved around to different countries. When his father's career was finished, the family moved to Regina, Saskatchewan and then to Victoria on Vancouver Island.

As Steve grew up he became a sport nut although he did not look like an athlete he excelled in everything he tried. His ability to analyse and process information were two of his greatest assets. Steve did have a natural skill for soccer but preferred to participate in lacrosse and rugby and loved to watch hockey. His favourite player was Wayne Gretzky, who was considered smaller than most hockey players, and Steve hoped that some day he would achieve the same success.

During the eighth grade, Steve discovered the game called basketball and played on an organized league. At that point in his life he told his mother that some day he would be an NBA star. While attending St. Michaels University School, Steve would not give up on his hoops dream. He worked on the skills of the game constantly and developed ankle-breaking quickness and was fearless going to the basket. Steve and his coach believed he could play major college basketball in the United States but others did not think the same way. His coach wrote and called more than two dozen colleges in the United States but the response was the same. "No Thanks!"

The only school that expressed any interest in Steve was tiny Santa Clara, a Jesuit University south of San Francisco. After viewing a video of Steve playing in a game, the assistant coach was impressed with his ability and told the Broncos coach Dick Davey. Davey flew to Canada to watch Steve play basketball in the British Columbia Senior Boys Triple A Championships. Davey was shocked to find out that he was the only American scout sitting in the stands. After the game, Davey met with Steve and offered him a school scholarship to Santa Clara and the opportunity to play with the Broncos on the condition that Steve focus on being a complete player. Davey told Steve that he was the worst defender that he had ever seen. For Steve that was not a problem as he was willing to do whatever he was asked.

Steve played for four seasons with the Broncos and when he graduated from Santa Clara he was chosen by the Phoenix Suns in the 1996 N.B.A. draft. Steve played for the Phoenix Suns until 1998 and was then traded to the Dallas Mavericks with whom he achieved greater success. In 2004, Steve became a free agent and returned to the Phoenix Suns. He played well for the team and was named MVP in one season, led the league in assists, and free-throws, and was ranked as one of the top players in the NBA League history in three point shooting and assists per game. He played for the team for eight years.

In 2012, Nash was traded to the Los Angeles Lakers. During the various playing seasons Nash has suffered from various injuries that have kept him from playing.

Steve Nash is well respected by his teammates and his fans. He has proven many times an old saying, 'One should never judge a book by its cover.'

SSR1135   ISBN: 9781771589659
© On The Mark Press

Image credit: Debby Wong / Shutterstock.com

Steve Nash
A Basketball Wonder

A READING
Complete the following sentences.

1. Steve's family moved around to different countries because _____

_____

2. The Nash family moved to Canada because _____

_____

3. To many people Steve Nash did not appear athletic because _____

_____

4. Steve Nash admired Wayne Gretzky because _____

_____

5. Dick Davey told Steve during an interview that he had to focus on becoming a complete player because

_____

6. Steve Nash did not get upset with Davey's criticism because _____

_____

7. Nash had a successful eight years with the Phoenix Suns because _____

_____

8. Steve's playing with the Los Angeles Lakers has been difficult because _____

_____

B LANGUAGE
Identify each underlined word's part of speech. Record their names on the line in order.

1. Steve Nash was a skinny kid who wanted to play basketball.

_____

2. Steve hoped that some day he would achieve the same success as Wayne Gretzky.

_____

3. The only school that showed any interest in Nash was a small one outside of San Francisco.

_____

4. Nash has not played as many games for the Los Angeles Lakers because of various injuries.

_____

C WORD STUDY
Locate words in the story that match each meaning.

1. very thin	_____	5. completed school	_____
2. did the very best	_____	6. very surprised	_____
3. to take part	_____	7. exchanged	_____
4. a high place of learning	_____	8. all the time	_____

SKILLS: Cause and Effect | Parts of Speech | Word Meanings   SSR1135 ISBN: 9781771589659
© On The Mark Press

Sidney Crosby
A National Hockey League Star

Sidney was born in Halifax, Nova Scotia on August 7, 1987 and was raised in Cole Harbour. At the age of three, he learned how to skate with his father and in no time he was playing organized hockey at the Atom Level. His father noticed that his hockey skills were excelling faster that his age.

- When Sidney was 13 he tried out and was picked for a major midget league for 16 to 17 year old boys. He made the team but was not allowed to play as the league felt he was too young so he returned to his bantam team. The next year he was allowed to play on the team and Sidney showed them how good he was by scoring 217 points and led the team to a second place finish in the Air Canada Cup.

- During his midget career, he was teased and taunted so often by the players and their parents that he would not wear his hockey jersey between tournament games so he wouldn't be recognized.

- When the NHL began showing interest in Sidney, his parents wanted him to improve and strengthen his skills. He was sent to a hockey driven prep school that was located in the state of Minnesota in the U.S.A. His parents hoped this school would help him to grow and mature as a person.

- The following year, Sydney was first overall pick in the midget draft by the Rimouski Oceanic Team of the Québec Major Junior Hockey League and began playing in the 2003-2004 season. At the end of his first season, Sydney had scored 54 goals and made 139 points in 59 games. He was named Player of the Year, Top Rookie, and Top Scorer and was the first player in the QMJHL League to earn all three awards.

- Sidney also participated in two World Junior Championship Tournaments. In 2004, he helped the team win a silver medal and in 2005, he participated again in the same tournament and scored 6 goals, had 3 assists, and helped Canada to win the gold medal. In 2005, Crosby was drafted by the Pittsburgh Penguins. In his first NHL season, Crosby finished sixth in league scoring with 102 points, 39 goals, and 63 assists and was runner up for the Calder Memorial Trophy. During his second season, Crosby led the NHL with 120 points, 36 goals and 84 assists and captured the Art Ross trophy becoming the youngest and the only teenager to win a scoring title in any major North American sports league. During the same season Crosby won the Hart Memorial Trophy for most valuable player and the Lester B. Pearson Award as the NHL Players Association Choice for most outstanding player. He was the 7th player in NHL history to earn all three awards in one year.

- In the 2007-2008 season, Crosby was made the Pittsburgh Penguins captain at the age of 20. During that year the Penguins played in the 2008 Stanley Cup finals but were defeated by the Detroit Red Wings in six games.

- Season 2008-2009 brought the Pittsburgh Penguins back to the NHL finals against the Detroit Red Wings again. This time the Penguins won the Stanley Cup in seven games. Crosby became the youngest captain in NHL history to win the Stanley Cup.

- During the 2009-2010 season, Crosby scored a career-high 51 goals and won the Mark Messier Leadership Award. The 2010-2011 season was not a good one for Crosby. He had a concussion as a result of hits to his head in back to back games. This injury kept him from playing for ten and a half months. Crosby's concussion-like symptoms returned in December of 2011 and he did not return to hockey until mid-March 2012 after having treatments by a special doctor. During 2013-2014 Sidney played well and has not been bothered with the effects of the concussion.

- Internationally, Crosby has represented Canada in numerous tournaments for Canada's junior and men's hockey teams. He played for Team Canada in the 2010 Winter Olympics in Vancouver where the team defeated the United States in the gold medal game by Sidney scoring the winning goal in overtime. In 2014, Crosby was the captain of the Canadian Olympic Hockey Team at the Sochi Olympics and led them to a gold medal victory over Sweden.

Sydney Crosby has had an impressive hockey career and has already been identified as one of NHL's greats!

SSR1135   ISBN: 9781771589659
© On The Mark Press

Image credit: photosthatrock / Shutterstock.com

Sidney Crosby
A National Hockey League Star

A **READING**

Complete the following activities.

1. Did Sidney Crosby have any problems being the youngest and very talented playing hockey?

_____

_____

_____

2. Why did his parents send him to a special hockey school in the United States?

_____

_____

_____

3. What did Crosby become at the beginning of the 2007-2008 NHL season?

_____

_____

4. Why was the 2010-2011 NHL season not a good one for Crosby?

_____

_____

5. Hockey can be a rough game that causes many major injuries to the players. Do you think that the games need to be so rough and hurtful to produce good hockey? Explain your answer.

_____

_____

_____

B **LANGUAGE**

Identify each underlined part of speech. Record their names on the line in order.

1. Sidney was often injured by other players when he first played hockey.

_____

2. His parents hoped this school would help him to grow and mature and to improve his hockey skills.

_____

3. As a young child, Sidney liked to fire pucks against the family dryer in the basement.

_____

C **WORD STUDY**

Locate the antonym or synonym for each of the following words.
Put an *S* or an *A* beside each pair of words.

1. major   _____ _____   5. rough   _____ _____

2. group   _____ _____   6. different _____ _____

3. end   _____ _____   7. ordinary _____ _____

4. weaken   _____ _____   8. lowered   _____ _____

SSR1135   ISBN: 9781771589659
© On The Mark Press

The De Havilland Beaver
A Northern Traveller's Dream

At one time, Canada's northern wilderness with its crystal clear lakes and countless forests could not be visited by anyone unless they used a canoe. People and companies needed a way to get in and out quickly and safely. In 1947, De Havilland Canada built the first bush plane for pilots and the military and called it the Beaver.

Read the following facts and find out more about bush planes.

- The Beaver was a plane that did not require a long air strip for landing and taking off

- Many people consider this tough, versatile plane the world's best bush aircraft.

- Many countries bought them for domestic and military purposes.

- It was used by the Americans during the Korean War who called it the 'general's jeep.'

- The Beaver could land on short runways using wheels, or skis and on water using pontoons.

- The Beaver could climb at a rate of 311 metres per minute even with heavy loads which enabled it to get in and out of small or narrow areas.

- It was made of metal and had a high lift wing 14.5 metres long and could travel 756 km in distance.

- The Beaver was powered by a 450 horsepower engine and was quieter than regular aircraft.

- The Beaver was the practical workhorse of pilots on rough terrain delivering goods and people to places without runways.

- When people wanted bigger and faster bush planes that had all the same features of a Beaver, De Havilland designed the powerful Turbo-Beaver, the larger Otter and Twin Otter and then the Caribou and Buffalo as newer engines became lighter.

- In 1966, the Canadian-built planes demonstrated landing and taking off from downtown New York to show off their STOL which is their short take off and landing abilities. This event demonstrated how it was possible to have downtown airports and shorter commuter flights.

- The Otter could land on a strip 300 metres long, carry nine passengers and a two-person crew. It was used by the Ontario Provincial Police Air Service, the R.C.A.F., Canadian Airlines, the U.S. Navy, and the U.N. Emergency Force in the Middle East. It even flew to the Antarctic.

- The Twin Otter is a larger version of the Otter. Twin Otters were used around the world in jungles, deserts, mountains, and the Arctic. They can land safely in the Arctic with their large balloon-like tundra tires which makes landing on soft ground possible and a landing strip is not needed.

- Today Twin Otters can carry twenty passengers safely to their destinations.

If you visit the Canadian Aviation Museum in Toronto you will be able to view the first 1947 prototype of the Beaver.

SSR1135   ISBN: 9781771589659
© On The Mark Press

The De Havilland Beaver
A Northern Traveller's Dream

A | READING
Which bush plane is each sentence describing?

The Beaver   **The Otter**   **The Twin Otter**

1. It was able to climb 311 metres per minute into the air when it was taking off. _____

2. This plane could land on an airstrip 300 metres long. _____

3. This plane was used to fly in and out of jungles, deserts, mountains, and the Arctic. _____

4. It is able to land using tundra tires, pontoons, and skis. _____

5. It can carry nine passengers and a two person crew. _____

6. This bush plane was able to transport twenty passengers. _____

7. Goods and people were transported to places without runways on this plane. _____

8. This plane was used by the police, the military, and the United States Navy. _____

B | LANGUAGE
Skim through the sentences in the story to locate and record two of each part of speech. Record the words on the lines.

1. Proper Nouns: _____

2. Common Nouns: _____

3. Verbs: _____

4. Phrases: _____

5. Adjectives: _____

6. Adverbs: _____

7. Prepositions: _____

8. Pronouns: _____

C | WORD STUDY
Add the correct vowel combination to each word.

ie   oo   ea   ai   ui   ou   ee

1. pont ____ ns
2. B ____ ver
3. ar ____ s
4. h ____ vy
5. j ____ p
6. ____ rcraft

7. cl ___ r
8. n ____ ded
9. b ____ lt
10. t ____ gh
11. wh ____ ls
12. qu ____ ter

13. terr ____ n
14. f ___ tures
15. ar ____ nd
16. m ____ nt ____ ns
17. ball ____ n
18. gr ____ nd

 SKILLS: Recalling Details | Parts of Speech | Vowel Combinations   SSR1135   ISBN: 9781771589659
© On The Mark Press

The Trans-Canada Highway
The World's Longest National Highway

The Trans-Canada Highway is like a ribbon of black silk winding its way across Canada.

The Trans-Canada Highway...

- is a highway made out of asphalt 7,821 km long.

- crosses the entire continent from west to east.

- is the longest national highway in the world.

- can be crossed nonstop in ten long days or two weeks with normal stops.

- has many interesting places and things to see along the way.

- connects St, John's, Newfoundland on the Atlantic Ocean to Victoria, British Columbia on the Pacific with the help of two ferry rides.

- travels through barren land, forests, fishing villages, farmlands, and past mines, lakes, cities, fields of wheat and spectacular mountains.

- runs west to east through all ten provinces.

- does not cross the three terrtories.

- has a green and white maple leaf for a logo on its signs.

- would have been a faster way to cross Canada than months travelling by horses, wagons or boat the way early settlers did

- construction was approved in 1949 by an act of Canada's parliament.

- was worked on and paid for by each province.

- was started in the 1950's and it was opened in 1962.

- brings tourists to Canada every year.

- was built by blasting rocks to clear a path, building bridges over rivers and streams, removing trees, and making firm roadbeds through dangerous swamps and muskeg.

- helps Canada's economy as many natural resources are carried to ports where they are shipped all over the world.

- was declared completed on September 3 in 1962 on Labour Day at Rogers Pass by Prime Minister Diefenbaker.

Today the Trans-Canada Highway is travelled on by cars, trucks, buses, motorcycles and bicycles delivering goods or viewing the breath-taking scenery in Canada.

SSR1135 ISBN: 9781771589659
© On The Mark Press

The Trans-Canada Highway
The World's Longest National Highway

A READING
Complete each sentence with the correct words from the story.

1. The Trans-Canada Highway is made of _____ and travels from St. John's, _____ to _____, British Columbia.

2. It is _____ km long and travels through _____ land, forests, _____, villages, and tall, snow-covered _____.

3. It does not _____ the three _____ in Canada's north.

4. Each _____ was responsible for the _____ and work on their _____ of the _____.

5. Workers _____ large rocks to _____ the way and built _____ over _____ and _____ .

6. The Trans-Canada Highway has a _____ and _____ maple _____ as its _____ on signs all along it.

7. The Trans-Canada Highway was _____ open in 1962 on _____ Day by _____ Minister John Diefenbaker.

B LANGUAGE
Underline the *adjectives* and circle the *adverbs* in each sentence.

1. The long, winding highway lazily wound its way around crystal clear lakes, tall mountains, and over bubbly rivers.

2. Early settlers slowly struggled across Canada over its rugged terrain.

3. The road workers had to carefully remove the huge rocks using dynamite.

4. The large bridge was eventually built over the fast-flowing, wide river.

C WORD STUDY
In the story locate three and four syllable words and record them on the chart below.

Three Syllable Words	Four Syllable Words
_____	_____
_____	_____
_____	_____
_____	_____
_____	_____
_____	_____

SSR1135 ISBN: 9781771589659
© On The Mark Press

The World's Tallest Totem Pole
A Beautiful First Nation Carving

Sitting at the north end of Cormorant Island on the outskirts of the village of Alert Bay in British Columbia stands a totem pole 53 metres tall. It is made of two large logs from the trunks of large trees called giant cedars found on the Northwest Coast. It was carved in the late 1960's by Jimmy Dick who was helped by Benjamin, Adam and William Dick, Gus Matilpe and Mrs. Billy Cook who are Namgis Nation artists. The carvings on the totem pole represent figures in the stories, beliefs, and legends of the Namgis First Nation.

How is a totem pole made?

- A tree is felled, the wood is debarked and then shaped using implements such as adazes, axes, chisels, carving knives and chain saws.

- Artists use these tools to create the swirling oval shapes common in First Nation artwork.

- After the wood has been carved, the pole may be painted or left natural.

Who carves a totem pole?

- Totem pole carvers begin carving at a young age and learn this skill from their fathers and uncles.

- Carvers are artistic but are also very familiar with the cultural history and the wood that they use.

- Years ago only the men carved totem poles but today women have become skilled carvers.

Why did First Nation People carve totem poles?

- Totem poles were monuments to honour their ancestors, history, people or events.

- Longhouses had house posts carved with human or animal forms to support the main beams in it.

- Some used a totem pole at the front of their long-house to tell about the family's history and wealth.

- Mortuary totem poles contained the remains of the dead person in a grave box and served as a tomb or headstone.

- A memorial totem pole was often created to honour an important dead person and it was usually the tallest type of pole.

- Some totem poles were called shame poles and were erected to ridicule neighbouring groups who had unpaid debts. Today, they are erected as a form of protest for political problems.

How long does a totem pole stay standing?

- Most poles are made from rot-resistant cedar trunks but most only last a hundred years and then they begin to fall apart.

What do the symbols on a totem pole mean?

The symbols are usually animals or birds.

The *Raven* is a bird that likes to play tricks.

The *Sea Turtle* represents Mother Earth.

A *Thunderbird* causes rolling thunder by beating its wings and creates lightening when it blinks its eyes. It is known to kill whales.

The *Eagle* is clever and rules the sky and can change itself into a human.

The *Wolf* is a very powerful totem who can help people that are sick or in need.

The *Bear* is a teacher symbol as the people believed it taught them how to catch salmon and to pick berries

The *Frog* brings wealth.

The *Otter* is mischievious and is a symbol of laughter, curiosity, grace, and empathy.

The *Salmon* is a symbol of instinct, persistence, and determination.

The *Owl* is a highly respected animal and represents the souls of the departed.

The *Killer Whale* represents all whales because they are strong and brave fish.

Stately poles tell many stories.

SSR1135 ISBN: 9781771589659
© On The Mark Press

The World's Tallest Totem Pole
A Beautiful First Nation Carving

A **READING**
Record the word 'True' or 'False' after each statement.

1. All totem poles are made the same size and have the same carvings. _____

2. The tallest totem pole in the world is found outside Alert Bay in British Columbia. _____

3. The carvings on the totem poles are faces of famous First Nation People. _____

4. Totem pole carvers know all about First Nation history and customs and the type of wood that they use. _____

5. Only men and boys learn how to carve totem poles. _____

6. Namgis artists use planes, hammers, nails, screwdrivers and drills while creating a totem pole. _____

7. All totem poles are painted very bright colours and look the same. _____

8. After a totem pole has been standing for one hundred years it begins to rot and fall apart. _____

B **LANGUAGE**
An *adjective phrase* modifies a noun and an *adverb phrase* modifies a verb.
Underline the adjective phrases and circle the adverb phrases in the sentences below.

1. Totem pole carvers begin carving at a young age.

2. The tallest totem pole in the world is found in British Columbia.

3. Trees of great size are carved to make totem poles.

4. The longhouse often had a totem pole at its front door.

5. Symbols of birds and animals are carved on the totem poles.

C **WORD STUDY**
Complete each word from the story with the correct blend or digraph.

sk   tr   kn   sw   cl   gr   st   cr   bl   sh   ch   th   wh   br   str

1. ____ unks	9. ____ oups	17. ____ ame
2. ____ ives	10. ____ anding	18. ____ under
3. ____ irling	11. ____ eates	19. ____ ave
4. ____ ill	12. weal ____	20. ____ isels
5. ____ ont	13. ____ inks	21. ____ ace
6. ____ ever	14. ____ ales	22. ____ ands
7. ____ ave	15. ____ ong	23. ____ ave
8. head ____ one	16. ____ aped	24. ____ ainsaw

SSR1135   ISBN: 9781771589659
© On The Mark Press

The Inventor of Insulin

Doctor Frederick Banting

Frederick Banting grew up on a farm near Alliston, Ontario. When he was a young man one of his friends named Jane, who was normally a very active girl, was tired all the time and ate more than she usually did and kept getting thinner and thinner. Then she became very sick and died of a disease called diabetes at the age of 14. Frederick became very confused and could not understand why some doctor had not invented a cure for this terrible disease that had caused Jane to suffer and die.

When Frederick grew up he went to university to become a doctor and researcher. He was especially interested in the body part called the pancreas, which is a gland behind the stomach. The pancreas treats the protein, starch, and fats we take into our bodies so they can be used to the best possible way. If the pancreas is not working, diabetes happens. Diabetes is the disease that causes an over supply of sugar in the blood.

During his research, young Dr. Banting found out that another researcher had discovered that the pancreas had little particles floating free like islands in it. They were called the 'Islets of Langerhans' after the doctor who discovered them. In a diabetic patient these islands shrivel up even though the pancreas is still healthy. Dr. Banting felt if there was some way to keep the islands healthy there should be hope for diabetic people who cannot properly digest and regulate sugars. In 1920, the only treatment for diabetes was a restricted diet.

Dr. Banting decided to research for a cure using dogs. He also needed a university laboratory, an assistant, and funds to support his research. Dr. John MacLeod allowed him to use his laboratory at the University of Toronto during his summer vacation. Dr. Banting was also given ten dogs, a research assistant named Dr. Charles Best, and eight weeks to prove his theory. It took nine months instead. The doctors were not paid and they often spent the night in the laboratory watching their patients.

One day, they operated on a dog who was dying of diabetes. Dr. Banting carefully removed the little islands from the dog's pancreas. Dr. Best then boiled them with water to make a serum and then it was injected into the dog's veins. For a little while nothing happened until the dog came out of the anesthetic. It then began to wake up, wagged its tail, and ran around. Banting and Best knew they were on the right path but they still had a long way to go in finding a cure. A skilled biochemist was brought in to refine and purify this serum called 'insulin' so it could be used on people.

On January 11 in 1922, Banting and Best had the opportunity to try their serum on a fourteen year old boy who was dying from diabetes. The boy was willing and his parents begged the doctors to try it on him. After the injection, the boy became alert, sat up, and felt good. The boy did recover and did not care if he had to take regular injections of 'isletin' later named insulin. The researchers were extremely happy and this was a triumph for medical history.

Today, this life-saving liquid is made from the glands of cows being slaughtered for market and is called insulin. For his work Dr. Banting won a Nobel prize in medicine in 1923.

The Inventor of Insulin
Doctor Frederick Banting

A READING

Answer each question with a sentence.

1. Why did Frederick Banting become interested in the disease diabetes?

_____

_____

2. Which part of the human body did Frederick find the most interesting as a young doctor?

_____

3. How does the pancreas help people?

_____

_____

4. What is diabetes?

_____

_____

5. How did Banting and Best know that the serum would work on people?

_____

_____

6. What is insulin made from today?

_____

_____

B LANGUAGE

Record the names of the underlined phrases on the line at the end of each sentence.

1. In the body behind the stomach is a gland called the pancreas. _____

2. Dr. Banting carefully removed the islets from the dog's pancreas. _____

3. Dr. Best boiled the islets with water to make a serum that was injected into the dog's veins.

_____

4. Frederick's friend Jane was the reason why he looked for a cure of the disease called diabetes.

_____

C WORD STUDY

Add the suffixes s, ed, ing to each of the following words.

1. name   _____   _____   _____

2. die   _____   _____   _____

3. confuse   _____   _____   _____

4. shrivel   _____   _____   _____

5. hope   _____   _____   _____

6. regulate   _____   _____   _____

SSR1135   ISBN: 9781771589659
© On The Mark Press

New Tools to Perform Body Functions
The Prosthesis

Years ago artificial limbs were made mainly for adults who had served in the two World Wars and had lost an arm or leg. Then in the 1950's and early 60's women were giving birth to babies with missing limbs. This was caused by a drug they had taken, called thalidomide, during pregnancy to relieve the feeling of being sick.

Their were so many children born without a limb or limbs at that time that members of the Variety Club in Toronto felt there was a need for a company to develop and produce artificial limbs for infants and children. In Toronto today, there is the Bloorview MacMillan Centre that is a leader in designing electric limbs for children.

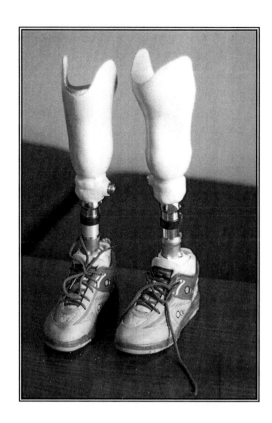

Many years ago, children with amputated arms or hands were fitted with hooks at the age of two or three. Attached to the hooks were cables the children used to operate them using their shoulder muscles. This is how they grasped and used objects. Very young children did not have the strength to operate this device. Today, children who have lost a hand in an accident or were born without a hand are fitted with one that is electric and has a strong grip and looks very much like a normal hand. Children as young as ten months can be fitted with electric hands and learn how to operate them. The earlier children are fitted with artificial limbs, the sooner they will adapt and skillfully operate them.

Each amputation for a child or adult is unique and the prosthetic limb must be custom fitted and then built. The person who designs and fits a prosthetic limb us called a prosthetist who requires skills in engineering, anatomy, and physiology. First the prosthetist takes precise measurements. Sometimes the measurements are done before the patient's limb is amputated. Once the amputation has been completed, the wound is healed, and the swelling has disappeared, a plaster mould is taken of the part that has been left. The mould serves as a template for making a duplicate of the remaining limb. The duplicate limb is used to test the fit of the prosthetic limb as it is being built. Care and attention is paid to the structure of the patient's remaining limb and the location of the muscles, tendons, and bones. After the prosthetic device is fitted, the patient must practise using it through physical therapy.

Most prothesis are powered by the person's body but electronic prothesis are becoming more popular. These limbs are controlled by a battery. They are operated by electric signals sent from the brain to muscles in the arm that tell the device how to move. Electrodes implanted in the prosthesis sit on the skin over certain muscles in the remaining part of the limb. As each muscle contracts individually the signal is recorded and made stronger in the prothesis which activates the motor that controls the hand. Most electronic hands can only open and close but finger movements are being developed.

The electronic leg prothesis uses a motor to control movement of the 'knee' joint. These muscles contract to tell the knee which way it should move. Sensors in the knee, lower leg, and prosthetic foot collect information about the position of the leg as the person moves.

Science has certainly made life better for disabled Canadian adults and children.

SSR1135   ISBN: 9781771589659
© On The Mark Press

New Tools to Perform Body Functions
The Prosthesis

A READING
Number the following sentences in the correct order.

_____ Sarah had to stay in the hospital for three weeks while waiting for the stump of her left leg to heal.

_____ Two weeks later a prosthetist came to her room carrying her prosthesis and showed her how to put it on and how to use it.

_____ One day in May, a nine year old girl named Sarah was walking home from school with her friends.

—— Then a prosthetist came into her room and announced that he was going to measure her good leg and to make a mould of it so her prothesis could be made.

_____ When she went back to school wearing her new leg her classmates hugged her and told her they missed having her involved in all of their activities.

_____ Suddenly a car veered off the road, mounted the sidewalk, and struck Sarah crushing one of her legs.

_____ Sarah practised walking with her new leg holding onto the parallel bars at first and then gradually on her own

_____ She was rushed to the hospital by ambulance where a doctor told her and her parents that she had to have her leg amputated below her knee.

B LANGUAGE
A word which names the receiver of the verb's action is called an *object of the verb*. e.g. The boy closed the *door*. The word door is a noun and object of the verb *closed*. Underline the verb and object in each sentence.

1. The girl lost her left leg.

2. Years ago hooks replaced hands.

3. Most prothesis are powered by the person's body.

4. Electric prothesis are becoming more popular.

C WORD STUDY
Record the root word for each of the following words on the line.

1. babies _____

2. electric _____

3. skillfully _____

4. fitted _____

5. measurements _____

6. amputation _____

7. implanted _____

8. information _____

9. disabled _____

10. controlled _____

SSR1135   ISBN: 9781771589659
© On The Mark Press

World War I Horses
Morning Glory: Canada's War Horse

During the years from July 1914 to November 1918 many countries were involved in a war to end all wars. Thousands of men and horses gave their lives during the many battles that they were involved in. In the early days battles were fought on horseback during cavalry charges. During World War I, trench warfare was used and soldiers stood in long, muddy trenches lined with barbed wire and used machine guns and rifles. This new type of warfare was too difficult for soldiers on horseback to charge and shoot at their enemy at the same time. In one charge of 150 men on a German trench only four survived. The rest were killed by machine gun fire.

Although the calvary charge was no longer a good method in trench warfare, horses were still needed to pull wagons loaded with food and supplies, large guns, and other equipment. These horses walked through hot sands in deserts, across deep rivers, and in very muddy places pulling these heavy loads. Many were often hurt or killed during their travels.

Many of the horses used during World War I were sent from Canada by ship. One of these horses was named Morning Glory and was owned by Lt. Col. George Harold Baker. She was shipped to England from Brome County in Québec's Eastern Townships in 1915. Her owner was a lawyer, a member of Parliament for Brome, and a part-time soldier for the reserves. When the war began, Baker volunteered to go overseas and when he travelled to England in 1915 by ship, Morning Glory went with him along with many other horses. Unfortunately, when they arrived in England, Baker and Morning Glory had to part company. Baker and his men had been reclassified as infantry and were sent to fight in the trenches. The horses were sent to France. Baker and Morning Glory never were together again as Baker was killed on June 2, 1916. He had gone to war thinking that he would be the leader of a cavalry charge on his horse Morning Glory instead he died in a muddy trench in Flanders during nonstop shellfire and was buried in Flanders Field.

Morning Glory was more fortunate than most horses who had to drag heavy guns and wagons through the mud while guns were firing and bombs were exploding. She was selected by a battalion commander who used her for his personal mount.

At the end of the war in 1918, Morning Glory was returned to Canada by General Dennis Draper, a close friend of Lt. Gen. George Baker. This was very unusual as most of the horses were left behind, mistreated or destroyed for their meat after the war. Morning Glory spent time on Draper's farm in Brome County and was used on Bill Coughtry's mail route to give her some exercise. Morning Glory received love and care from many local people and lived a peaceful life in Québec. She died in 1936 at the age of 26 and is buried behind the Baker's summer home near Baker pond.

Morning Glory was a faithful charger who served her time in the war.

SSR1135 ISBN: 9781771589659
© On The Mark Press 85

World War I Horses
Morning Glory: Canada's War Horse

A **READING**

Tell why each event happened in the story.

1. Cavalry fighting was not used in World War I.

_____

_____

2. Horses were still used during the war.

_____

_____

3. Morning Glory and Lt. Col. George Baker had to part company in England.

_____

_____

4. Baker and Morning Glory never saw each other again.

_____

_____

5. Morning Glory was better off than most horses during the war.

_____

_____

B **LANGUAGE**

Record the name of the parts of speech on the lines under each sentence.

Bare Subject	Bare Predicate	Object

1. The world was involved in a war.
   B.S. _____ B.P. _____ O. _____

2. Soldiers fought in deep, mucky trenches.
   B.S. _____ B.P. _____ O. _____

3. War horses walked through very dangerous places.
   B.S. _____ B.P. _____ O. _____

4. Morning Glory was loved by the people in Brome Country.
   B.S. _____ B.P. _____ O. _____

C **WORD STUDY**

Locate words in the story that match each meaning.

1. soldiers who fought on horseback   _____

2. a long, deep, narrow, ditch   _____

3. to suddenly attack an enemy   _____

4. to offer one's services freely   _____

5. to have good luck   _____

6. a large organized fighting group   _____

Big Ben

Canada's Show Jumping Hero

Big Ben was born on a farm in Belgium and was first named 'Winston' after the famous British Prime Minister Winston Churchill. In 1983, an owner of a farm in the Netherlands bought him and renamed him 'Big Ben' because he looked tall like a clock tower. No one wanted to buy him because they felt he was too big and ugly looking. Big Ben stood 17.3 hands high.

On a trip to the Netherlands while visiting Emile Hendrix, a friend, Ian Miller learned about a seven year old, chestnut coloured, Belgian warmblood. He went to see the horse and knew quickly that this was the horse he had to have. Millar purchased Big Ben for $45,000.00 and had him shipped to Miller Brooke Farm near Perth, Ontario.

Miller took Big Ben to Florida for the winter along with his other show horses. It was here that Miller discovered he had an extremely talented horse when he began training him. In no time a bond was formed and in 1984, Big Ben and Millar began competing in show jumping events. During Big Ben's first Grand Prix appearance, the pair came second. A week later, at the Grand Prix at Spruce Meadows in Alberta, they won their first of many Grand Prix titles. During the same year at the Los Angeles Olympics, Ian and Big Ben helped the Canadian Equestrian Team to finish in fourth place.

In 1987, Millar and Big Ben won the individual and team gold medal at the Pan American Games in the United States. Miller and Big Ben continued to have success and in 1989, Miller was voted to be 'Male Athlete of the Year' and was given the title 'Captain Canada.' Ian Miller and Big Ben were now celebrities.

During 1990, while in Florida, Ben began to show signs of having colic and had to be operated on. The operation went well and many hoped Big Ben could still compete. The team showed all was well by winning at Spruce Meadows and had three more Grand Prix wins. In 1991, ten months after his first colic attack, Big Ben had to undergo surgery again for a second colic attack. Many were doubtful that he would ever compete again. During the winter, he returned to Florida where the warm weather and the sunshine helped him to recover quickly. When he returned to Canada, the team won two World Cup qualifiers in Calgary and Ottawa. Millar and Big Ben received a standing ovation from the audience at Spruce Meadows as it was incredible that at that level of competition a horse could compete after surviving two colic surgeries.

In 1992, Big Ben was involved in a highway accident. The driver of a minivan had fallen asleep at the wheel and had hit Big Ben's trailer head on. The driver of the van was killed and when the horse trailer swerved it tipped over and fell into a ditch. One horse died, two were badly injured and one was very frightened. Big Ben was rushed to a hospital where he received stitches to close a huge gash over one of his eyes. After this disaster, Big Ben went on to Calgary where he competed and won all three classes and took home the $100,000.00 Shell Cup.

In 1993, at the age of 17, Big Ben had one more successful year in show jumping. He won the title of Canadian National Showjumping Champion and won the $100,000.00 Shell Cup again. In 1994, Millar decided it was time that his faithful partner of eleven years be retired. Millar took him across Canada during shows to let people and children see Big Ben up close. In 1999, Big Ben was the second horse to be inducted into the Canadian Sport Legends Hall of Fame. Northern Dancer being the first. Big Ben's image was also put on a postage stamp as well. On December 11, 1999 at the age of 23, Big Ben had his third bout of colic and had to be euthanized.

Today at Millar Brooke farm, Big Ben rests on a grassy knoll that overlooks the farm and fields where he lived and played. In downtown Perth, in a park beside the Tay River is a statue of Ian Millar and Big Ben jumping. It is a beautiful statue that was erected in his memory.

Big Ben will always be remembered as the horse with a great heart.

Big Ben
Canada's Show Jumping Hero

A **READING**

Complete the following activities.

1. Write a description of Big Ben in a paragraph using good sentences.

_____

_____

_____

2. Tell why you think Ian Miller picked Big Ben while others did not like him.

_____

_____

3. Tell how Big Ben proved to people that Ian Miller had made the right choice in horses.

_____

_____

4. How did Big Ben prove he was in good form after his first bout with colic?

_____

5. Why did the audience honour Big Ben and Ian Miller at Spruce Meadows with a standing ovation?

_____

_____

6. What other incident took place in Big Ben's life that could have ended his career?

_____

_____

B **LANGUAGE**

Record the names of the parts of speech on the line under each sentence.
Is it Bare Subject, Bare Predicate or Object?

1. Big Ben spent the winters in Florida.
   BS. _____ B.P. _____ O. _____
2. Miller went to see the horse.
   B.S. _____ B.P. _____ O. _____
3. The horse was born on a Belgian farm.
   B.S. _____ B.P. _____ O. _____
4. Miller and Ben made a strong jumping team.
   B.S. _____ B.P. _____ O. _____

C **WORD STUDY**

Locate the words in the story that match each meaning. Record them on the lines.

1. well known _____   5. severe pains in the stomach _____

2. bought, paid for _____   6. loud clapping, cheering _____

3. has natural ability _____   7. painless death _____

4. a strong feeling _____   8. people who watch a show _____

SSR1135   ISBN: 9781771589659
© On The Mark Press

The Newfoundland Dog
A Gentle Giant

One of the largest dogs bred in Canada is the Newfoundland often nicknamed the 'Newf, Newfie, or Gentle Giant.' They were bred at first as working dogs to help fishermen on their boats. The Newfoundland is known for its size, intelligence, tremendous strength, calm nature, and its loyalty The female Newfie may weigh 60 to 70 kg and the male 99 to 121 kg. Its coat is thick and straight and may be black, brown, beige, have black and white patches or be grey in colour which is the rarest kind.

The Newfoundland has large bones and powerful muscles that enables it to swim through rough ocean waves and powerful tides. Its large lungs allows the Newfie to swim long distances. Its thick, oily coat and waterproof double undercoat helps to keep it warm in very cold, icy waters. The Newfoundland's feet are large, strong, and webbed and make it easy for it to travel over marshes, sandy shores, and to swim.

The Newfoundland is at home on land and in the water. There are many stories about Newfoundland dogs that have rescued men and women from watery graves, carried life lines to shipwrecks, and have rescued children who have fallen in deep water. Newfoundlands are also working dogs who helped fishermen with their heavy nets and other tasks on their boats. Although the Newfoundland is a superior water dog it is also used to pull loaded carts or to carry loads on its back like a pack horse. This is often seen in Newfoundland and Labrador today. Most Newfies are kept as pets, companions, and guard dogs.

Read the following Newfoundland rescue stories:

- In Holland one day, a man was walking with his large Newfoundland along the edge of a dike. His foot hit a slippery spot causing him to lose his balance and fall into the water. He could not swim and soon became unconscious. When he woke up he found himself in someone's cottage. The farmer who owned the cottage told him he saw a large dog swimming and dragging something in the water. When the dog pulled his owner out of the water the farmer realized it was the body of a man and got help for him.

- A man walking on the bank of the river Tyne saw a child falling into it on the opposite side. He gave a command to his Newfoundland who immediately jumped into the river and swam quickly to the struggling child. The Newfoundland grabbed the child's coat with its mouth and swam to shore.

- Gander was a Newfoundland dog that showed bravery and courage during World War II. He accompanied a battalion of Canadian soldiers to fight against the Japanese on Hong Kong Island. When the Japanese soldiers landed on the beach near the Canadian soldiers, Gander would bravely stand and bark at them and try to bite their legs. Another time Gander protected a group of wounded soldiers by charging and barking at Japanese soldiers who changed their direction and never attempted to shoot Gander or the wounded soldiers. Gander's greatest and last act of bravery took place during a battle. An enemy grenade landed near a group of soldiers. Gander quickly grabbed the grenade in his mouth and carried it away. Unfortunately the grenade exploded in Gander's mouth killing him instantly.

Many a Newfoundland dog has been a hero.

SSR1135   ISBN: 9781771589659
© On The Mark Press

The Newfoundland Dog
A Gentle Giant

A **READING**

Complete each sentence with words from the story.

1. Because the Newfoundland has strong muscles and webbed feet _____
   _____

2. Because it has a thick, oily, outer coat and a waterproof double undercoat _____
   _____

3. Because it has large lungs _____
   _____

4. Because its feet are webbed the Newfoundland _____
   _____

5. Newfoundlands were bred _____
   _____

6. Because it is a large strong dog the Newfoundland is also used _____
   _____

7. People like to have a Newfoundland for a pet because _____
   _____

8. Newfoundlands are courageous dogs because _____
   _____

B **LANGUAGE**

Identify each underlined part of speech on the line below the sentence.

1. The <u>Newfoundland</u> has <u>large</u> bones and powerful <u>muscles</u>.
   _____

2. Its <u>webbed</u> feet can <u>easily</u> travel <u>over</u> <u>marshes</u> and <u>sandy</u> beaches.
   _____

3. The Newfoundland <u>carried</u> the life line <u>between</u> its teeth in its <u>mouth</u> to the people <u>sitting</u> in the <u>lifeboat</u>.
   _____

4. The Newfoundland called <u>Gander</u> was a <u>hero</u> <u>during</u> the second world war.
   _____

C **WORD STUDY**

Record the root words for each of the following words on the line provided.

1. largest	_____	6. marshes	_____
2. loyalty	_____	7. stories	_____
3. rarest	_____	8. owners	_____
4. enables	_____	9. slippery	_____
5. unfortunately	_____	10. struggling	_____

SSR1135   ISBN: 9781771589659
© On The Mark Press

Percé Rock

A Canadian Wonder

Percé Rock is a huge rock formation found in the Gulf of the St. Lawrence on the tip of the Gaspé Peninsula in Québec. From a distance it looks like a ship under sail. Here is a local legend that tells about a tragic love story that took place near the rock for you to read.

A young, handsome French Officer from France, named Raymond, fell in love and became engaged to a beautiful girl called Blanche. Unfortunately Raymond was assigned to a regiment in New France and was posted to the Fortress of St. Louis, in Québec. Blanche missed Raymond so much she decided to travel to Québec in New France to marry him.

Unfortunately during her journey the ship was attacked by Spanish pirates near Newfoundland. All the crew were killed by the pirates and their ship was gutted. Blanche, who had hidden in one of the cabins on the ship was discovered and dragged out and presented to the pirate captain. Upon seeing Blanche, the pirate captain fell in love with her and proposed marriage. Blanche agreed but she had other plans in her mind. During the wedding celebrations, Blanche suddenly jumped off the ship into the deep sea water and drowned. Suddenly the ship was surrounded by a thick fog and Blanche could not be rescued and sailing was difficult so the ship anchored for the night.

In the morning, the crew was surprised to see a huge rock facing them that seemed to be floating near the shore. Then suddenly the image of the girl called Blanche appeared on the rock waving her fist and cursing them. The crew tried to turn the ship to avoid the rock but crashed into it and the apparition disappeared. The next day, people who saw the rock said it had the appearance of a ship under sail.

Below are some real facts for you to read about Percé Rock:

- It is a massive rock cliff made of reddish-gold limestone and shale.

- A sandbar which is visible at low tide connects the rock to the mainland.

- It has steep faces on all sides and is 433 metres long, 90 metres wide, and 88 metres high.

- Percé Rock has one of the world's natural arches located in water. Its arch is 15 metres in height.

- It was named by the French explorer Samuel de Champlain.

- The arch is wide enough to let a small ship pass through it at low tide.

- People are able to walk to it during low tide on a sandbar but must be careful.

- Birds, such as silvery gulls, black cormorants, and gannats like to perch on top of it.

- Percé Rock is gradually getting smaller due to erosion and scientists claim it will disappear in 16,000 years.

- It contains many different types of fossils.

SSR1135 ISBN: 9781771589659
© On The Mark Press

Perçé Rock
A Canadian Wonder

A READING

Number the sentences about the legend in the correct order.

_____ One of the pirates found Blanche hiding in a cabin and presented her to the captain.

_____ The next day the crew faced a huge rock with the ghost of Blanche on it and crashed into it.

_____ Raymond and Blanche fell in love and became engaged to be married.

_____ One day her ship was attacked by pirates who killed the entire crew.

_____ When the pirate captain saw her he fell in love and wanted to marry her.

_____ Blanche missed him so much she decided to sail to New France to marry him.

_____ During the wedding celebration Blanche jumped overboard and drowned and couldn't be saved because a fog had suddenly surrounded the ship.

_____ Raymond went unhappily to New France by ship.

B LANGUAGE

An *adverb* is a word that describes a verb, an adjective or another adverb. Circle the adverbs and underline the words that they describe in each sentence.

1. The ship sailed quickly over the waves.

2. People walked carefully on the sandbar to get a closer look at the rock.

3. The waves slapped the rock very hard.

4. Extremely rough water makes the ship rock from side to side.

5. Blanche suddenly jumped off the ship and drowned.

C WORD STUDY

Complete the following activities.

1. Look for words in the story that have four syllables. Record them on the lines.

_____

_____

_____

2. Look for synonyms in the story for the following words. Record them on the lines provided.

a) trip _____   f) quickly _____

b) large _____   g) prevent _____

c) ghost _____   h) look _____

d) huge _____   i) kinds _____

e) seen _____   j) joins _____

SSR1135   ISBN: 9781771589659
© On The Mark Press

Niagara Falls
One of Nature's Wonders

When you visit Niagara Falls and stand by the railing to view one of nature's most beautiful sights a roaring sound is heard and cold mist-like spray hits your face as huge amounts of water pour over a high cliff. There are three waterfalls to view. They are the Horseshoe Falls, the American Falls, and the Bridal Falls.

Read the interesting facts below to find out more about Niagara Falls.

1. It is one of the seven wonders in the world.

2. There are three waterfalls to visit. The falls on the Canadian side is called the Horseshoe Falls and on the American side is the American Falls and the Bridal Falls.

3. The Horseshoe Falls is the largest, the American Falls is smaller, and the Bridal Falls is the smallest.

4. The three waterfalls straddle the international border between Canada and the United States or you could say Ontario and the state of New York.

5. The three waterfalls form the southern end of the Niagara Gorge on the Niagara River which drains Lake Erie into Lake Ontario.

6. The three falls have the highest flow rate of any waterfalls in the world and are the most powerful in North America.

7. The three falls were formed when glaciers receded at the end of the last ice age.

8. More than 168,000 metres of water falls over the crest of the Horseshoe Falls every minute which produces valuable hydro electric power.

9. The Mohawk nation claim the falls got their name from a Mohawk word 'anyara' which means 'neck' and is pronounced 'O - ne - au - ga - rah.' This term refers to the neck or portage route between lakes Erie and Ontario.

10. The Rainbow Bridge carries people and vehicles back and forth between the two countries.

11. Niagara Falls on the Canadian side is a beautiful place to visit. It has many gardens and parks, souvenir shops, restaurants, observation towers, museums and casinos. The Maid of the Mist boats will take you on the Niagara River and up close to the falls where the roar is louder and the spray heavier and colder.

12. Many daredevils have tried to or have gone over the Horseshoe Falls in barrels. Some survived while others drowned or were seriously injured. Some have gone over the falls without any protection and survived. Daredevils such as William Hunt and Blondin performed crazy stunts on a tightrope across the gorge many years ago

13. On June 12, 2012, high wire artist Nick Wallenda became the first person to walk across the falls in 116 years. His tightrope was 550 metres long and crossed near the top edge of the Horseshoe Falls while others had crossed farther downstream.

SSR1135   ISBN: 9781771589659
© On The Mark Press

Niagara Falls
One of Nature's Wonders

A READING
Locate the sentences that have the information to answer the following questions. Record its number on the line at the end of the question and record the first three words of it.

1. What do the three waterfalls form? _____

2. When were the three waterfalls formed? _____

3. How many waterfalls are found at Niagara Falls? _____

4. What are the names of the three waterfalls? _____

5. What is the size of each waterfall? _____

6. Which countries do the falls separate? _____

7. Why are the falls so famous? _____

8. How have daredevils travelled over the falls? _____

B LANGUAGE
Rewrite each sentence on the lines putting in the capital letters and punctuation.

1. the three falls are called the horseshoe falls the american falls and the bridal falls

_____

2. people travel between canada and the united states on the rainbow bridge

_____

3. did you know niagara falls got its name from a mohawk word

_____

C WORD STUDY
Complete the following activities.

1. Locate seven compound words in the story. Record them on the lines.

_____

_____

2. Locate nine words that have double consonants. Record them on the lines.

_____

_____

3. Locate the antonym for each of the following words in the story. Record the words on the lines.

a) under _____   f) hotter _____

b) front _____   g) short _____

c) lighter _____   h) bottom _____

d) softer _____   i) far _____

e) ugly _____   j) less _____

SKILLS: Finding Proof | Capitalization/Punctuation
| Compound Words | Double Consonants

SSR1135 ISBN: 9781771589659
© On The Mark Press

Hoodoos and the Alberta Badlands
Stunning Natural Wonders

One of Alberta's famous tourist attractons is to visit the Alberta Badlands to see the hoodoos.

Did you know that:

- a badland is a dry area where the rich soil has been worn away by wind and water.

- canyons, ravines, gullies and hoodoos are found in the Badlands.

- plants and trees cannot grow in Badland areas.

- the Big Muddy Badlands was a place where outlaws would hide in caves.

- a hoodoo located in the Alberta Badlands is usually 10 to 15 metres high and made of sandstone. On top of the sandstone pillar is a cap of hard rock that keeps the softer sandstone from eroding

- the hoodoos in the Alberta Badlands are made from sand and clay.

- the hoodoos in the Alberta Badlands look like mushrooms. The solid capstones protect the softer base.

- the minerals inside different kinds of rocks cause the hoodoos to have different colours.

- hoodoos were formed by the effects of erosion caused by water, wind, and frost.

- some hoodoos in deserts have a 'totem pole' shaped body.

- hoodoos range in size from that of an average human to heights higher than a ten storey building.

- in the Badlands many dinosaur bones have been discovered.

- the hoodoos in the Badlands took millions of years to form.

- the Badlands were covered with lush jungles and shallow seas 75 million years ago.

- the valley where the Badlands are found has some of the hottest temperatures in Canada.

The eerie shapes of rocks and land make the Badlands a spooky place to visit.

SSR1135   ISBN: 9781771589659
© On The Mark Press

Hoodoos and the Alberta Badlands
Stunning Natural Wonders

A **READING**
Record *true* or *false* on the line in front of each statement about hoodoos or the Badlands.

_____ 1. Tropical jungles and grasslands are found in the Badlands.

_____ 2. The Badlands contain ravines, gullies, and hoodoos.

_____ 3. Some of the hoodoos in the Badlands look like very tall totem poles.

_____ 4. The wind, water, and frost formed the hoodoos in the Badlands.

_____ 5. The Badlands have always looked dry and barren.

_____ 6. Minerals in the rock causes hoodoos to have different colours.

_____ 7. The Badlands are very cold all of the time.

_____ 8. Different types of plants can be found growing in the Badlands.

B **LANGUAGE**
'And', 'or', and 'but' are called *conjunctions*. They join words or parts of sentences together. Complete each sentence with the correct conjunction.

1. Wind _____ water has worn away the rich soil in the Badlands.

2. Some hoodoos are as tall as a totem pole _____ as high as a ten storey building.

3. Today the Badlands are dry and worn _____ at one time they had lush jungles and seas.

4. The Badlands have canyons, gullies _____ ravines.

C **WORD STUDY**
The word 'hoodoo' has the 'oo' sound. Record and spell other words with the same sound to answer each clue.

1. The name of a horse's foot. _____

2. To go very fast. _____

3. A small stream. _____

4. A person who steals. _____

5. Scary, frightening. _____

6. A house made of snow. _____

7. An animal with big horns. _____

8. Used for stirring _____

SSR1135   ISBN: 9781771589659
© On The Mark Press

The Rideau Canal
UNESCO World Heritage Site

The Rideau Canal is the oldest, still operating, canal system in North America. It connects the city of Ottawa, Ontario on the Ottawa River to the city of Kingston.

Here are some interesting facts about it:

- The canal system uses parts of major rivers and lakes such as the Rideau and Cataraqui Rivers and the Lower and Upper Big Rideau Lakes.

- The Rideau Canal was built for military purposes. During the War of 1812 the Americans planned on invading the British Colony in Upper Canada using the St. Lawrence River. Forts were also built along it.

- It was also built to provide a secure supply and communication route between Montreal and the British Naval Base in Kingston. It also bypassed the part of the St. Lawrence River that bordered the state of New York.

- The construction of the canal was supervised by Lt. Col. John By and most of the work was done by thousands of Irish and French-Canadian labourers.

- Many labourers died from malaria and other diseases and accidents during its building.

- The work on the canal began in 1826 and it took six years to complete by 1832.

- The canal was never used for a military route as Canada and the United States were at peace.

- It was used to ship logs, timber, minerals, and grain to different places. It served as the main travel route for British Settlers heading west to Upper Canada.

- Today it is used mainly by pleasure boats and tour boats who use the canal to travel from one place to another. It takes three to five days to travel one way through the Rideau Canada System by boat.

- Most of the locks are hand operated to let water in or out.

- There are 45 locks at 23 stations along the canal.

- Gates let boats in and out of each lock. The water level is lowered or raised by a lock master.

- In the winter, the section of the Rideau Canal that passes through central Ottawa becomes the world's largest skating rink. Its surface is 7.8 km long. It's open 24 hours a day from January to March. It is a popular tourist attraction and it is where the Winterlude Festival is held.

The Rideau Canal is a Canadian Heritage River.

SSR1135   ISBN: 9781771589659
© On The Mark Press

The Rideau Canal
UNESCO World Heritage Site

A READING

Answer the following questions.

1. List the ways the Rideau Canal was used in the past.

_____

_____

_____

2. How is the Rideau Canal used today?

_____

_____

3. How long did it take to build the Rideau Canal? Why do you think it took so long?

_____

_____

4. Who helped to build the Rideau Canal?

_____

_____

5. Why did so many labourers die while working on the canal?

_____

_____

6. Why was it never used as a military route?

_____

_____

B LANGUAGE

Follow the directions given for each sentence.

1. Underline the **nouns**.   Many labourers died from maleria, other diseases and accidents.

2. Underline the **verbs**.   Logs, timber, and minerals were shipped to different places.

3. Underline the **adjectives**.   It served as a main travel route for British settlers heading west.

4. Underline the **adverbs**.   The water in the lock slowly and steadily raised our boat.

C WORD STUDY

Record the root word for each of the following words.

1. planned   _____   6. largest   _____

2. invading   _____   7. attraction   _____

3. using   _____   8. labourers   _____

4. settlers   _____   9. served   _____

5. operated   _____   10. communication _____

SSR1135   ISBN: 9781771589659
© On The Mark Press

Québec City
A Historic Canadian Place

Québec City is one of the oldest cities in North America and was founded in 1608 by Samuel de Champlain. It is the capital city of the province of Québec and has a population of 765,706. Its name comes from an Algonquian word 'kebec' which means 'narrowing of the water'.

Read the following facts about this interesting and famous city:

- Québec City has some of the oldest buildings in North America.

- It is a city that has maintained the French language and customs.

- Walls surrounding Old Québec make it the only fortified city remaining in the Americas, north of Mexico.

- Old Québec City was declared a World Heritage Site by UNESCO in 1985 and was named the Historic District of Old Québec.

- Upper Town in Québec City is located on a beautiful site on top of a cliff overlooking the St. Lawrence Seaway. It is defended by walls with bastions. A bastion is a part of the wall that projects out and was used to hold canons. The Citadel is a star-shaped fortress made of 25 buildings and is a military museum.

- Lower Town is located near the harbour and has old living quarters and homes built close to cobblestone streets.

- Thirty sets of stairs and a funicular (a kind of train or trolley) link Upper Town and Lower Town. Breakneck Stairs built in 1635 contains 59 steps and is the city's oldest stairway. Camp Blanc Stairs has 398 steps and is the city's longest staircase.

- Chateau Frontenac is in Upper Town and is one of the most photographed hotels in the world. It is also one of the tallest buildings in Québec City.

- Near the Chateau Frontenac is a boardwalk that takes you along the St. Lawrence River. Along the boardwalk are cannons to remind us of the city's history.

- The Plains of Abraham is the place where a battle was held between the British led by General James Wolfe and the French led by the Marquis de Montcalm. The British won the battle and the French lost control of New France (Canada). Both leaders died from wounds they received during the battle. Today the Plains of Abraham make a very large park.

- Sainte-Anne-de-Beaupre Shrine is visited by many people each year. It is a large church with hundreds of stained glass windows and has a beautiful interior. Outside the Shrine is a golden statue of Sainte Anne.

- Montmorency Falls is a beautiful sight to see. It is a waterfalls that is 83 metres high and is taller than Niagara Falls by 30 metres. When you stand close to it you can feel the force of its spray.

Be sure to visit Québec City and step back in time.

SSR1135   ISBN: 9781771589659
© On The Mark Press

Québec City

A Historic Canadian Place

A **READING**

Look for details in the story that are answers to the following questions.

1. Where is Upper Town located in Québec City?

_____

_____

2. Why is Québec City the only fortified city in the Americas north of Mexico?

_____

3. Where did the city get its name and what does it mean?

_____

_____

4. What building in Québec City is famous around the world?

_____

5. How are Upper and Lower Town connected?

_____

_____

6. Where did a famous battle take place?

_____

7. What place in Québec is visited often by tourists?

_____

B **LANGUAGE**

Record the name of the part of speech underlined in each sentence.

1. A bastion is part of the wall that holds canons. _____

2. Chateau Frontenac is a tall stately building often photographed. _____

3. One must slowly and carefully walk up and down the thirty sets of stairs. _____

4. The Shrine is a large church with stained glass windows. _____

5. When you stand close to Montmorency Falls you feel the force of its spray. _____

C **WORD STUDY**

Look in the story for antonyms, synonyms or homonyms of the following words.

1. sight   (H) _____   7. highest (S) _____

2. newest   (A) _____   8. lead   (H) _____

3. widening (A) _____   9. one   (H) _____

4. stares   (H) _____   10. boring (A) _____

5. planes   (H) _____   11. fight   (S) _____

6. close   (S) _____   12. port   (S) _____

SSR1135 ISBN: 9781771589659
© On The Mark Press

The R.C.M.P. Academy and Heritage Centre
Canada's Early Police Force

Canada's R.C.M.P. are known all over the world for their colourful uniforms and their musical ride on beautiful black horses. This police force began on August 30 in 1873 when Canada's parliament passed an act to establish a Police Force called the North West Mounted Police after the massacre of many of the Assiniboine Nation at Cypress Hills. Their role was to bring law and order to the West, drive out whiskey traders and outlaws, to establish friendly relations with the First Nation People, and to ensure the safety of railway workers and new settlers.

In 1876, Sitting Bull, a Sioux chief, fled into Canada to hide from the America military after he defeated General Custer and the 7th Cavalry at the Little Big Horn. N.W.M.P. Inspector James Walsh had to ride into a camp of 5000 Sioux warriors to tell Sitting Bull that he must obey Canada's laws. This was one of the brave deeds performed by an early N.W.M.P. officer.

Today in Regina, you can visit the R.C.M.P. Academy or Depot that trains young people to become officers in the force and the R.C.M.P. Heritage Centre to see interesting sights and artifacts from the past. Below are some of the things that you can see and visit.

- In the summer, the Sergeant Major's Parade and Sunset Retreat Ceremony are two events that mark the end of the training day at the R.C.M.P. Training Centre. The cadets are dressed in Scarlet tunics, black boots, and their special hats and march to the music played by bagpipes and the beat of a snare drum. You will hear canons roar and silence while the Canadian flag is lowered, folded, and retired for the night.

- Buildings at the Academy may be visited. The Chapel is the oldest remaining building in Regina. On each side of the altar is a stained glass window portraying a member of the force. On one side is an R.C.M.P. in mourning and on the other side is a trumpeter sounding reveille.

- At the R.C.M.P. Heritage Centre there are many artifacts and displays to see and visit.

- There are displays of different kinds of equipment, weapons, uniforms, photographs, and exhibits with famous historical people.

- In the exhibits you will find Chief Sitting Bull and Louis Riel.

- Items on display include First Nation artifacts and clothing and a large painted buffalo skin with pictures of Canadian history.

- Historical items such as Louis Riel's handcuffs and the crucifix he carried to the gallows are on display.

- In another display is a captured spy's uniform, pen microphone, and chemical-tipped matches.

- Other items on display are the gifts given by Chief Sitting Bull to Inspector James Walsh. They are a combined tomahawk and peace pipe, a decorated rifle case and a tobacco pouch.

- The snowshoes of the Mad Trapper of Red River can be seen in a display. He always wore them backwards to fool the Mounties so he would not be caught.

The Heritage Centre tells how important the R.C.M.P. were in the peaceful settling of the western provinces.

SSR1135 ISBN: 9781771589659
© On The Mark Press

The R.C.M.P Academy and Heritage Centre
Canada's Early Police Force

A READING
Answer the following questions with sentences.

1. Why was a police force needed in the western part of Canada?

_____

_____

2. What brave act did Inspector James Walsh perform?

_____

_____

3. What does the R.C.M.P. Academy do in Regina?

_____

_____

4. Why is the Heritage Centre an important place to visit?

_____

_____

5. Name several things that you may see if you visit the Heritage Centre.

_____

_____

_____

6. What two ceremonies, performed by R.C.M.P. cadets, do people enjoy watching at the training centre?

_____

_____

B LANGUAGE
Underline each *phrase* and circle each *object* in the sentences.

1. The N.W.M.P. were to bring law and order to the west.

2. The R.C.M.P. cadets march to bagpipe music and the beat of a snare drum.

3. In one display I saw the uniform of a spy.

4. Sitting Bull and his warriors fled to Canada to hide from the American cavalry.

C WORD STUDY
Using a dictionary locate and record the meanings of the following words.

1. massacre: _____

2. establish: _____

3. relations: _____

4. artifacts: _____

5. portray: _____

6. historical: _____

7. gallows: _____

8. combine: _____

SKILLS: Recalling Details | Parts of Speech | Word Meanings   SSR1135 ISBN: 9781771589659
© On The Mark Press

A Mennonite Heritage Village
Early Settlers of Manitoba

- **Who were the Mennonites?**
  The Mennonites were a group of people who left the Roman Catholic Church many years ago while living in countries in Europe

- **In which countries did the Mennonites first live?**
  They lived in Russia, Germany, the Netherlands, and Switzerland.

- **Why did they leave their homeland?**
  They were not liked by other people because of their religious beliefs, the way they lived, and their feelings about fighting in wars.

- **Why did the Mennonites choose to settle in Canada?**
  They were promised land, the freedom to keep their lifestyle, and they were also exempt from military service.

- **Where did the Mennonites settle in Canada?**
  Some settled in Ontario but many chose to live in the western provinces of Manitoba and Saskatchewan.

- **How do the Mennonites prefer to live today?**
  Some live in a modern way while others still cling to their traditional way of life, dress, and travel.

- **What type of work did the Mennonites prefer to do?**
  They liked and enjoyed farming.

- **How did the Mennonites improve the way of life in early Western Canada?**
  They were the first settlers to build shelters on the prairie called sod houses. They also introduced fruit trees, the sunflower, and the watermelon to Manitoba. They built windmills and later steam mills to grind wheat into flour for Canada and other countries. The Mennonites were the first farmers to grow wheat in large fields.

- **Where can I visit a Mennonite Village in Manitoba?**
  There is a fantastic Mennonite Heritage Village near Steinbach, Manitoba.

- **What buildings will I be able to visit?**
  People like to visit the *Semlin* which is a house made out of sod, soil, and wood.
  The *Hochfield House* is an early log dwelling that was built in a Mennonite village.
  The *Chortitz Housebarn* was used for the family to live in and a place to keep their animals.
  The *Peters Barn* is 121 years old and was able to take the harsh winds and cold of the prairie and kept the animals warm. At the *Sawmill Shelter* you may see old machines that cut wood and make shingles. Near the centre of the village you will find a plain building called the *Old Colony Worship House*. Inside you will find rows of hard wooden benches. It is a Mennonite church. Many homes had a summer kitchen and an **outdoor oven** to cook in. This helped to keep the house cool in the hot weather. The outside oven was used to make bread. It is also fun to visit the *Farm Barn and Animal Pens* to watch the types of animals kept on a Mennonite farm. At the Heritage Village there are 33 different things to see. Some are buildings, monuments, statues, old farm machinery and even an old windmill.

Visiting the Heritage Village will take you back in time so you can imagine life in an early settler village.

SSR1135 ISBN: 9781771589659
© On The Mark Press

A Mennonite Heritage Village
Early Settlers of Manitoba

A READING
Complete the following questions.

1. Record a few facts that you learned about the Mennonites in a paragraph.

   _____

   _____

   _____

2. Tell how the Mennonites improved life in the western provinces.

   _____

   _____

   _____

3. Why do you think people use old buildings and old items to make heritage villages?

   _____

   _____

4. Put a check mark beside the activities you may see being done at a heritage village.

   ☐ milking a cow   ☐ churning cream into butter   ☐ a tractor plowing
   ☐ someone putting clothes into   ☐ making wax candles   ☐ grinding wheat into flour
     a dryer   ☐ using a power lawnmower   ☐ animals in a pen
   ☐ riding a bike   ☐ someone weaving on a loom   ☐ someone making a quilt
   ☐ someone loading a   ☐ spinning wool into yarn   ☐ a woman making bread
     dishwasher

B LANGUAGE
Write the following kinds of sentences about the Mennonite Heritage Village.

1. Interrogative: _____

   _____

2. Imperative: _____

   _____

3. Assertive: _____

   _____

4. Exclamatory: _____

   _____

C WORD STUDY
Record (H) for homonyms, (S) for synonyms, and (A) for antonyms after each word pair.

1. plane, plain _____   4. leave, return _____   7. wood, would _____

2. hard, soft _____   5. modern, traditional _____   8. near, close _____

3. group, crowd _____   6. flour, flower _____   9. outdoor, indoor _____

SKILLS: Recalling Facts | Kinds of Sentences
| Antonymns, Homonyms, Synonyms

SSR1135   ISBN: 9781771589659
© On The Mark Press

Fort Henry – Kingston
A Popular Military Museum

Fort Henry is located on Point Henry which is near the mouth of the Cataraqui River where it flows into Lake Ontario. The original fort was built in 1812 to protect the Kingston Royal Dockyards from an attack by the United States. The present fort was rebuilt between 1832 to 1837 to protect the Rideau Canal from being attacked by the United States. Both forts were never attacked.

Today Fort Henry is a tourist attraction. Visitors can watch soldiers being trained, the Changing of the Guard, Sunset Ceremonies, a Performance by the Fort Henry Guards, and the Drill Squad and Artillery Detachment perform in military drills to marching bands topped off by a mock battle with rifle and cannon fire. Visitors can also meet the fort's mascot, a goat called David X while touring the fort.

Read the following facts about some of the places you can visit at the fort.

- The **Advanced Battery** has a group of guns called cannons that face the lake to protect the fort.

- A **Dry Ditch** that is 40 feet wide and 30 feet deep is found along the inside walls. Soldiers could shoot enemies who got over the wall from the fort's 302 rifle loopholes in the inner wall.

- **Garrison Cells** were used for bad soldiers who had broken rules or had gotten drunk or committed crimes such as desertion.

- The **Privies** are open toilets used by the men and soldiers. They did not have seats. The Privies with seats were used by the officers and women.

- The **Officer Quarters** were used by officers who came from upper and middle class British families. They had to pay for their own food, equipment, and their own position in the army. The commander ran the fort from his quarters but usually lived in a house with his family.

- The **Ante Room** was where the officers played games, relaxed or entertained people.

- The **Soldiers' Barracks** were made up of large rooms. In each room 18 men slept, ate, and spent their free time. The beds were small and could fold up. Under each bed was a box for the soldiers own things. These rooms were poorly lit and heated and had no windows for light and fresh air. At night the rooms were locked on the outside so soldiers could not desert the army.

- The **School Room** was used by the children of soldiers. They were taught by a schoolmaster and a school mistress. They went to school for six days of the week. Sometimes soldiers used the room at night to learn about things.

- Families lived in the **Married-Quarters**. Each family had one quarter of a barrack's room. In each area were two beds where the parents slept. The children slept on the floor. Curtains separated the four areas at night for privacy.

- The **Bakery** was the place that baked the bread for the fort. The ovens could bake 120 loaves of bread at one time. Each soldier received a one and a half pound loaf of bread daily.

- The **Powder Magazine** is a large room with shuttered windows. At one time it could hold 1,250 kegs of gun powder.

- The **Cookhouse** prepared meals for the common soldiers. They were made in large pots used to boil food and to make soups and stews.

Visiting Fort Henry is like travelling through part of Canada's history.

SSR1135   ISBN: 9781771589659
© On The Mark Press

Image credit: SF photo / Shutterstock.com

Fort Henry – Kingston
A Popular Military Museum

A   READING
Which part of the fort is each sentence describing? Record its name on the line.

1. Officers often played games and met people in this room. _____

2. Wonderful smells drifted out of its ovens early in the day. _____

3. Eighteen men slept, ate, amused themselves in this part at night. _____

4. The commander of the fort only used this area while he was working. _____

5. Children spent many days and hours in this room. _____

6. This was a very dangerous room that held harmful material. _____

7. Soldiers who broke rules and tried to run away were kept in this area. _____

8. A family lived in one quarter of a room. _____

B   LANGUAGE
Pretend you are a child living in Fort Henry. Write a paragraph about an exciting event that took place.

_____
_____
_____
_____
_____
_____
_____
_____
_____
_____

C   WORD STUDY
Locate words in the story that have a pair of double consonants and match the following meanings.

1. a room used for soldiers to sleep in _____

2. a large gun that shoots large metal balls _____

3. soldiers who are in charge of the fort _____

4. part of the fort that faced the lake _____

5. a group of soldiers in a fort _____

6. closed up windows _____

7. practising in a group _____

8. fighting, warfare _____

SKILLS: Main idea | Paragraph Writing | Double Consonants

SSR1135   ISBN: 9781771589659
© On The Mark Press

The Calgary Stampede
The Greatest Outdoor Show on Earth

In July of every year, the city of Calgary, Alberta hosts its annual rodeo, exhibition, and festival. One million people visit it each year. The Calgary Stampede consists of a large parade, a midway, stage shows, concerts, farming competitions, a rodeo, chuckwagon racing and First Nations displays and shows.

Learn more about the Stampede by reading the following facts.

- The Calgary Stampede began in 1886 as an agricultural fair. In 1912, Guy Weadick, an American promoter held his first rodeo and festival called the Stampede in Calgary. In 1923, Weadick's Stampede and the Calgary Exhibition joined hands to create the Calgary Exhibition and Stampede.

- Calgary is a well-known city around the world and is often called the 'Stampede City' or 'Cowtown.'

- Everyone in the city wears western gear such as denim blue jeans, plaid shirts, a white cowboy hat, a leather belt with a large buckle and cowboy boots made from cowhide, rattlesnake, python, or alligator skin and other hides.

- Hundreds of pancake breakfasts and barbeques are held throughout the city.

- The Stampede begins with a huge parade on the first Friday of the event. It is led by a parade marshall followed by dozens of marching bands, over 150 floats and hundreds of horses with riders. Some are ridden by famous people, cowboys, First Nation people, and the R.C.M.P. in their colourful uniforms.

- The heart of the Stampede is the rodeo which is the largest and most famous event of its kind in the world. Cowboys perform in bull riding, barrel racing, steer wrestling, tie-down roping, saddle bronco and bareback riding. The competitors all compete to win prize money.

- The Rangeland Derby is exciting chuckwagon racing which is very popular. Thirty-six teams compete for 1.5 million dollars in prize money. The wagons used are like the ones used years ago to supply meals to cowboys who were out on the range. Each wagon is pulled by four horses with a driver and is followed by four mounted outriders. The race begins with a tight figure eight manoeuvre that has to be completed by all wagons before they burst onto the track for a dash to the finish. Teams compete for prize money.

- In the agricultural buildings people can view farming products, farming methods, the history of grain growing on the prairie and how bread, cereals and other wheat products are made.

- During the evening, people can sit by the Coca-Cola Stage to watch and listen to concerts performed by famous country performers and the Calgary Stampede Showband.

- At the Midway there are 35 different types of rides including the swing tower, mega drop, the spinning coaster, the giant wheel and many more.

- At the First Nations Village colourful tepees used by Plains people can be seen. Inside the tepees Plains people show how they cut meat, dry jerky and pemmican, do beadwork, bake bannock, and make clothing from animal hides. There are daily pow-wows, First Nation singing and dancing and other contests.

The Calgary Stampede brings thrills to all ages.

SSR1135 ISBN: 9781771589659
© On The Mark Press Image credit: xlibber, via Wikimedia Commons   107

The Calgary Stampede
The Greatest Show on Earth

A READING
Answer each question and give a good reason for your feelings.

1. If you could attend the Calgary Stampede, what part would you like to see? Tell why.

_____

_____

2. How do you feel about the way animals are used at the Calgary Stampede? Explain your feelings.

_____

_____

3. Which rodeo event do you think is the most dangerous for the rider? Tell why.

_____

_____

4. How do you know the citizens of Calgary are proud of their Stampede?

_____

_____

5. What part of the Calgary Stampede do you think most people like the best? Tell why.

_____

_____

6. Which rodeo event would you not like to watch? Tell why.

_____

_____

B LANGUAGE
Write a paragraph about watching your favourite rodeo event.

_____

_____

_____

_____

_____

C WORD STUDY
Unscramble the letters to make words found in the story. Record them on the lines provided.

1. o o r d e   _____

2. e a p a r d   _____

3. y m d a w i   _____

4. d p e e m s t a _____

5. c b b k a a e r _____

6. s t c c n o r e _____

7. s h o s r e   _____

8. s b y c o o w   _____

9. i i e p r r a   _____

10. n a c p i m m e _____

11. o a f s m u   _____

12. t c m o e p e   _____

SSR1135   ISBN: 9781771589659
© On The Mark Press

Québec Winter Carnival
Largest Winter Festival in the World

The Québec Winter Carnival has been the largest Winter Festival in the world for 56 years. It is 17 days of fun for all the families and people who visit it. The Carnival takes place from the middle of January to the middle of February in Québec City. There are many activities people can do, sights to see, and events to watch.

Read about some of the things you would see or could do at the Québec Winter Carnival.

- There are two parades to watch. One takes place during the day and the other one can be seen at night. The day parade has fifteen or more giant characters blown up and filled with helium. Bands play music and entertainers do things to make people smile. The night parade is filled with colourful floats, bands playing music and people wearing costumes. Leading both parades is a large snowman wearing a red toque and a colourful sash called Bonhomme.

- Bonhomme is a guest of honour and official mascot of the Winter Carnival. His home is the Ice Palace. The Opening and Closing Ceremonies are held here along with many other events.

- People can snowshoe or cross-country ski on the many trails at a park called the Plains of Abraham. Another popular activity at the park is to ride the zip line high above it.

- Outdoor racing events take place in different parts of Québec City. There is a sleigh race across the Plains of Abraham Park. Horses pulling sleighs with drivers race to see which team is the fastest.

- On the St. Lawrence River there is a canoe race on freezing cold water filled with large chunks of ice floating on it.

- Another popular event is dogsled racing on the snow covered streets of Old Québec City. Here 30 teams show their skills while racing over 6 km.

- Sculptors carve things out of blocks of ice and snow in competitions. Some are seen on the streets or are displayed in a large tent.

- There is a fair grounds with bouncy houses, a large ferris wheel and an ice slide. There is also snow rafting down snow covered hills.

- Horse pulled sleighs take visitors on rides to maple sugar shacks to get a dollop of maple sugar poured on the snow where it hardens quickly.

- People also stop to buy a beavertail. It is a delicious kind of doughnut that is flat and shaped like a beaver's tail.

- People often take the ferry to a town called Levi and back to cross the St. Lawrence River to see the chunks of ice.

- There are many more sights, events, and places to visit at the Québec Winter Carnival.

What a wonderful way to celebrate winter!

SSR1135   ISBN: 9781771589659
© On The Mark Press

Image credit: Mariday

Québec Winter Carnival
Largest Winter Festival in the World

A **READING**

Answer each question with a sentence.

1. Where and when is the Québec Winter Carnival held?

_____

_____

2. How long has this festival been taking place?

_____

3. Who is the guest of honour and mascot at the Québec Winter Carnival?

_____

4. Where is Bonhomme's home at the Québec Winter Carnival?

_____

5. List the names of some of the competitions that people can watch.

_____

_____

6. When do the parades take place at the festival?

_____

_____

7. What two treats do visitors like and enjoy eating?

_____

_____

B **LANGUAGE**

Write a paragraph about Bonhomme. Describe his appearance and what he does.

_____

_____

_____

_____

_____

_____

C **WORD STUDY**

Skim through the story to find the antonyms for the following words.

1. summer	_____	6. low	_____
2. smallest	_____	7. pushing	_____
3. night	_____	8. slowest	_____
4. frown	_____	9. sinking	_____
5. following	_____	10. softens	_____

SSR1135   ISBN: 9781771589659
© On The Mark Press

The Santa Claus Parade
The World's Finest Christmas Parade

In 1950, when I was nine years old and my sister was seven, our parents took us by car to Toronto to watch the Santa Claus Parade. We were very excited as we had never been to Toronto or had we ever seen the Santa Claus Parade. When we arrived in Toronto, we hurried along Yonge Street and found a good spot near the T. Eaton's Store. The air was filled with excited voices as people lined up on both sides of the street. Others stood inside buildings and watched through the windows. The day was bright and sunny but very cold.

In the distance we could hear music playing and we knew that Santa was on his way. The floats that passed by were colourful and different sizes. The bands played cheery Christmas music. There were many people dressed as clowns, nursery rhyme and storybook characters and last of all came Santa and his eight reindeer. He waved to the crowd and then entered the store where he would sit in his big chair in Toyland. Our parents took us to Toyland to sit on Santa's knee so we could tell him what we would like for Christmas. Toyland was a child's wonderland and was filled with toys of all kinds, shapes and sizes. My sister and I walked around it in wonder and surprise. The entire day was so exciting that as soon as we got in the car and our father began driving home, my sister and I feel fast asleep and dreamed of Christmas Day.

Did you know?

- The first arrival of Santa Claus to Toronto was in 1905 by train. He then was driven by car to the T.Eaton's Store. On the way he handed out souvenirs and surprise packages to children.

- In 1906, Santa arrived in a coach drawn by four white horses.

- In 1913, Santa was pulled down Yonge Street by a team of eight live reindeer brought in from Labrador. Men dressed in animal costumes walked beside the real animals.

- In 1917, the parade featured seven floats carrying nursery rhyme characters and Mother Goose appeared for the first time.

- In 1919, Santa arrived in the city by plane.

- In 1951, the parade consisted of 13 large floats and 20 smaller ones along with 2000 adults and children.

- In 1952, the parade was broadcast on the television for the first time in Canada and the United States.

- In 1953, Santa stood on a float that had a sleigh and eight white reindeer leaping over housetops.

- In 1982, the president of the T. Eaton Company announced that they could no longer sponsor the parade because of their problems with money.

- Businesses stepped in to save the parade and it is now sponsored by companies such as McDonald's, Canadian Tire, Lowes, Tim Hortons and others.

- In 2004 the parade had been going for 100 years.

- Today the parade has 25 floats, 24 bands, and 1700 participants

- The parade route is 5.6 km long.

- It is one of the biggest productions in North America and the oldest annual parade.

Watching the Toronto Santa Claus parade is a wonderful adventure for young children!

SSR1135 ISBN: 9781771589659
© On The Mark Press

Image credit: JStone / Shutterstock.com | mikecphoto / Shutterstock.com

The Santa Claus Parade
The World's Finest Christmas Parade

A READING
Tell when each of the following events took place.

1. A plane flew Santa Claus to Toronto. _____

2. The T. Eaton Company could no longer sponsor the parade. _____

3. The parade had seven floats with nursery rhymes and Mother Goose. _____

4. Santa arrived in a coach drawn by four white horses. _____

5. The parade celebrated its one hundredth birthday. _____

6. The parade was broadcast on television for the first time. _____

7. Santa Claus was pulled down Yonge Street by eight real reindeer. _____

8. The Santa Claus parade had 13 large floats, 20 small floats, and 2000 people. _____

B LANGUAGE
Write a paragrph describing today's Santa Claus Parade.

_____

_____

_____

_____

_____

_____

_____

_____

_____

_____

C WORD STUDY
Locate the antonyms, synonyms, and homonyms for the following words in the story.

1. fake (A) _____

2. ate (H) _____

3. plain (H) _____

4. same (A) _____

5. rushed (S) _____

6. left (A) _____

7. road (S) _____

8. emptied (A) _____

9. shorter (A) _____

10. pulled (S) _____

SSR1135   ISBN: 9781771589659
© On The Mark Press

ANSWER KEY

Section 1
CANADIAN HISTORICAL SITES

STORY #1: L'ANSE AUX MEADOWS; PAGE: 8

A. 1. L'Anse Aux Meadows is an early Viking Settlement.
2. It is located at the northern tip of Newfoundland and Labrador.   3. Helge Ingstad and his wife Anne Stine Ingstad examined the remains of this settlement.
4. The buildings were wooden structures covered with sod.   5. All that remains are ankle-high mounds of grass.   6. People can visit the Interpretation Centre to watch a movie about its history, look at artifacts found and view reconstructed Viking Scenes. Outside they can view the site of the first settlement and then visit the reconstructed Viking buildings and watch people dressed in Viking clothes.   7. The Knarr is a 16 metre long, hand made boat made of wood and iron rivets that came from Greenland.

B. 1. In 1960, L'Anse Aux Meadows was discovered by Helge Instade and his wife Anne Stine Helge from Norway.
2. The Knarr is a 16 metre Norse merchant ship that was built in Greenland and brought to L'Anse Aux Meadows by a crew of nine.

C. 1. discovered   2. constructed   3. dwellings   4. trail
5. imagine   6. reconstructed   7. demonstrate   8. craft

STORY #2: DAWSON CITY; PAGE: 10

A. 1. Gold was discovered in the Yukon.   2. Joseph Ladue founded the town and George M. Dawson explored and mapped it.   3. Gold was discovered in 1896 and this discovery began the Klondyke Gold Rush.
4. The Klondyke Gold Rush had ended.   5. The Alaskan Highway that was built bypassed Dawson City and went to Whitehorse   6. It is linked by a road to Alaska and one that goes to Whitehorse. Modern mining methods has made mining gold more profitable. The tourism industry has grown.   7. Jack London Museum, Cabin of Robert Service, Palace Grand Theatre, S.S. Keno, walking trails, historic creeks, gold rush camps, Diamond Gertie's Gambling Hall

B. Underlined Words: people, children, team, choir, dozen, family, army

C. 1. east   2. earlier   3. quickly   4. famous   5. ended
6. increased   7. oldest   8. beautiful

STORY #3: FORT MACLEOD; PAGE: 12

A. 1. what, where   2. who, what, where, why   3. what, where, why   4. when, who, what, where, why, how
5. who, what, where, why, when   6. what, how, who

B. Common Nouns: visitors, river, dwellings, fort, town, museum cliff, island, buffalo   Proper Nouns: Fort Macleod, Alberta, Calgary, Blackfoot, Manitoba
Collective Nouns: troupe, group, government, police, family, class, herds

C. 1. hour   2. led   3. main   4. time   5. plains   6. scene
7. wood   8. site   9. made   10. meat

STORY #4: PIER 21 CANADIAN MUSEUM OF IMMIGRATION; PAGE: 14

A. 1. Answers will vary   2. Possible answers: finding a job, a place to live, speaking the language, being understood, getting to know Canada's laws and rules, having enough money   3. Answers will vary.   4. Answers will vary.
5. Answers will vary.   6. Answers will vary.

B. 1. boarding   2. travelling   3. spoiled   4. discovered
5. fleeing   6. decayed   7. disembark   8. processed

C. 1. dislike or hatred for Jews; predjudice against Jews
2. hatred or fear of foreigners or strangers   3. the belief that one race, especially your own, is better than other races   4. a very strong dislike, loathing, ill will, malice

Section 2
FAMOUS HISTORICAL CANADIAN MEN

STORY #1: LOUIS RIEL (1844-1885); PAGE: 16

A. 1. He felt the Métis had the right to protect their lands from the government. Answers will vary.   2. The Métis and First Nation People were annoyed with the number of English Protestant settlers moving into their settlement. The Hudson Bay Company was selling the control of Rupert's Land to Canada and Ottawa was taking over.   3. He led a protest that stopped the surveyors and set up a temporary government and captured Fort Garry.   4. The message sent to McDougall was not received in time and Riel captured the attackers.   5. The government made the Red River Settlement the province of Manitoba but Riel and his followers lost their pardons and were hunted down.
6. Dumont told Riel the same thing that happened in Manitoba was also happening further west and the Métis and Plains Indians needed his help.   7. A battle took place and Dumont's men were outnumbered and defeated.   8. He was tried for treason and hung in 1885. They made Louis Riel a hero for all people to respect.

B. 1. talked (past tense)   2. knew (past tense)   3. begin (present tense)   4. wants (present tense)

C. 1. territories   2. lands   3. buffaloes   4. lives
5. families   6. communities   7. ideas   8. heroes

STORY #2: BILLY BISHOP (1894-1956); PAGE: 18

A. 1. he tried to fly his homemade plane.   2. he preferred outdoor activities such as hunting and riding.   3. they hoped the school's discipline would improve his marks.
4. he felt his bad behaviour would cause him to be expelled.   5. he wanted to get out of the stinking, muddy trenches.   6. he attacked a German airfield early

one morning and destroyed seven planes.   7. they were often shot down in their first three weeks of flying.   8. he had excellent vision and could spot enemy formations on the ground.
B. 1. Exclamatory   2. Assertive   3. Interrogative
4. Imperative
C. 1. activities   2. bullets   3. trenches   4. studies
5. enemies   6. members   7. victories   8. bombs

STORY #3: TIMOTHY EATON; PAGE: 20

A. 1. Possible answers: hard-working; apprenticed as a store owner; changed the way people paid for things; changed the way things were sold; used newspapers for advertisements; developed a mail-order business, etc.   2. He would not allow tobacco products or playing cards to be sold in his stores.   3. His stores closed earlier than other stores. He gave his employees Saturday afternoons off in the summer so they could spend time with their families. He would help employees who were sick or needy.   4. Answers will vary.   5. Answers will vary.
B. 1. Timothy Eaton worked as a shopkeeper's apprentice.   2. Timothy and his brothers opened up a dry goods store.   3. Robert Simpson became Timothy Eaton's competitor.   4. Hundreds of people flocked to the new T. Eaton store.
C. 1. haggling   2. emigrate   3. exhausted   4. donated
5. famine   6. clever   7. support   8. promoted

STORY #4: SIR JOHN A. MACDONALD (1815-1891); PAGE: 22

A. 1. 1873   2. 1847 - 1854   3. 1854   4. 1812-1891   5. 1847   6. 1867   7. 1891   8. 1843
B. 1. John A. Macdonald/**lived** in Glasgow.   2. His father/**ran** a store.   3. John/**needed** money for his family.   4. Queen Victoria/**knighted** John A. Macdonald.
C. 1. a person learning a trade or skill.   2. an officer of the government who has power to apply the law and put it into force   3. a shameful act; disgrace; shocks public opinion   4. the joining of a group of provinces or states to form a country   5. a political party opposing the party in power.

STORY #5: ROBERT SAMUEL MCLAUGHLIN (1871-1972); PAGE: 24

A. 1. the largest manufacturer of horse drawn buggies and sleighs in the British Empire.   2. youngest son   3. moved to the city of Oshawa   4. one carriage every ten minutes   5. Sam and his brother partners in the carriage company   6. designing a line of cars   7. Sam McLaughlin put his two companies together as one   8. He donated money to build a library, an art gallery, Camp Samac, Lakeview Park, and the Oshawa General Hospital
B. Underlined phrases: 1. of paint   2. to ride his horses; to compete; in many horse-jumping competitions   3. In 1934; of the Queen's Plate   4. of horses; to the building; of Parkwood Stables; from Oshawa

C. 1. experiences, experienced, experiencing   2. announces, announced, announcing   3. develops, developed, developing   4. manufactures, manufactured, manufacturing   5. designs, designed, designing   6. completes, completed, completing

STORY #6: JOSIAH HENSON (1789-1883); PAGE: 26

A. 1. Possible Answers: beaten, whipped, ears cut off, sold, families were split up   2. Josiah was the strongest, smartest, and most faithful of all of his owner's slaves.   3. He became a Christian, preached to his people and developed strong feelings about the unfairness and cruelty of slavery.   4. Answers will vary.   5. He created a Black Settlement called Dawn near Dresden. At the settlement the people were trained in skills they needed in order to survive.   6. She told Josiah Henson's story in her book called 'Uncle Tom's Cabin.'
B. 1. badly, beaten   2. be set, correctly, healed properly   3. hid quietly   4. moved silently, carefully
C. 1. antonyms   2. synonyms   3. synonyms   4. antonyms   5. synonyms   6. homonyms   7. antonyms   8. homonyms   9. synonyms   10. synonyms

STORY #7: WALTER ROLLING (1873-1943); PAGE: 28

A. 1. present   2. past   3. present   4. past   5. present   6. present   7. past   8. present   9. present and past   10. past
B. 1. to, near   2. to, for   3. at, in   4. into, with, in
C. 1. at-tend-ed   2. po-si-tion   3. prin-ci-pal   4. rep-u-ta-tion   5. pre-sent-ed   6. sur-vive   7. com-mun-i-ty   8. pre-ced-ed

STORY #8: JOHN WARE (1845-1905); PAGE: 30

A. Sequential Order: 2, 3, 1, 6, 4, 8, 5, 9, 7
B. Underlined adjectives and adjective phrases: 1. large; of cattle; northern   2. experienced; northern; ranching   3. remarkable; wildest   4. second; of logs; higher
C. 1. respect   2. ranch   3. marry   4. company   5. fear   6. mark   7. wild   8. territory   9. fortune   10. care

STORY #9: ELIJAH MC COY (1843-1929); PAGE: 32

A. 1. They were slaves escaping from Kentucky to live in Canada.   2. He had fought in the Upper and Lower Canada Rebellion.   3. Elijah went to study engineering.   4. He couldn't find a job in his field in Ontario.   5. The hot, high pressure steam can rust most metals and prevent them from moving .   6. The engines had to be lubricated.   7. His lubricator used steam pressure to pump oil wherever it was needed.   8. They were impressed with his invention.
B. Circled words: 1. we, it   2. He   3. Many   4. They, him
C. 1. unhook   2. disarm, forearm   3. forehead   4. disobey   5. midair   6. return   7. redo, undo   8. extraordinary

 SSR1135 ISBN: 9781771589659
© On The Mark Press

STORY #10: LINCOLN ALEXANDER (1922-2012); PAGE: 34

A. 1. 1953   2. 1942   3. January 21, 1928   4. 19535. 1965
6. 1965   7. 1968 to 1980   8. September 20, 1985
9. January 21   10. 2013   11. 1968   12. 1980
B. 1. Compound   2. simple   3. simple   4. compound
C. 1. passion   2. human   3. govern   4. point
5.compensate   6. culture   7. educate   8. feat
9. judge   10. point

Section 3
FAMOUS HISTORICAL CANADIAN WOMEN

STORY #1: LAURA SECORD (1775-1868); PAGE: 36

A. 1. Cause: Her mother died. Effect: She had an unhappy childhood.   2. Cause: Thomas Ingersoll heard that Upper Canada was giving away land. Effect: He made money so the family could settle on the land.
3. Cause: They wanted to remain loyal to Britain. Effect: Laura Ingersoll and James Secord met, fell in love, and married.   4. Cause: The United States had declared war on Britain. Effect: James was injured in a battle at Queenston Heights.   5. Cause: Laura had to warn Lieutenant Fitzgibbon about the 500 soldiers that were coming to destroy him and his men. Effect: Laura had to walk miles over muddy roads, through fields, and swampy areas.   6. Cause: In front of him was a dirty, tired, and bedraggled woman who was determined he believe her story. Effect: He took a chance and decided to act on her warning.   7. Cause: They were trapped by First Nation Warriors and soldiers who made them surrender. Effect: The Americans had lost a major battle and Fitzgibbons was promoted.
B. Checked Pronouns: he, them, she, him, they, his
C. 1. born   2. Ingersoll   3. American   4. tavern
5. Secord   6. first   7. farm   8. merchant   9. store
10. horrible   11. injured   12. returned   13. darkness
14. warrior   15. efforts

STORY #2: LUCY MAUD MONTGOMERY; PAGE: 38

A. 1. She had no one to play with until she went to school so she invented imaginary friends. She loved books and was able to read at a young age.   2. Possible Answers: missed the lifestyle on the island; didn't know her father very well; might not have liked her stepmother; missed her relatives; Prince Albert was so different than the island.   3. She continued to write stories, poetry and articles for newspapers and magazines.
4. Her grandfather Macneill died and she had to give up teaching to care for her grandmother Macneill. Answers will vary.
5. She spent a year in Halifax working at a newspaper as a writer and proof reader.   6. The writing of Anne of Green Gables and all of the sequels and having them published.
B. 1. adjective   2. Proper Noun   3. verb   4. adverb
C. 1. die   2. sent   3. real   4. write   5. been   6. marry
7. serial   8. eight   9. knew   10. site   11. wrote   12. role

STORY #3 MOLLY BRANT (1736-1796); PAGE: 40

A. 1. could speak English and Mohawk; went to school to learn how to read and write; showed interest in Iroquois politics; grew up in a European atmosphere; ran her husband's business when he was away; looked after the house and its household   2. acted as a spy for the British; stayed in her home to help Loyalists and her people to escape to Canada   3. She helped the Mohawk people her entire life and many Loyalists to escape
4. She dressed as a Mohawk woman while living in an European community called Cataracqui which is now Kingston   5. Answers will vary.
B. Underlined words: 1. She   2. They   3. them   4. He
5. I , them
C. 1. wealthy   2. visitors   3. allies   4. seized
5. numerous   6. battle   7. establish   8. pillaged
9. problems   10. ambushed

STORY #4 MARY ANN SHADD (1823-1893); PAGE: 42

A. Sequential Ordering: 4, 5, 1, 8, 2, 3, 6, 9, 10, 7
B. 1. what   2. who   3. whose   4. which   5. whom
C. 1. respectable   2. slavery   3. abolished   4. fugitive
5. segregation   6. settlement   7. discrimination

STORY #5: ANNA HAINING (SWAN) BATES (1846-1888); PAGE: 44

A. 1. hired, owner, work, museum   2. tourists, streets, asking   3. weighed, born, grew, quickly   4. waist, times, waist, women   5. museum, derrick, lowered, block, tackle   6. furniture, specially, comfortably   7. children, died, size   8. promoter, Martin Bates, team, sensation
B. 1. This   2. That   3. Those, this, that   4. This, these
C. 1. weigh   2. feet   3. waist   4. stairs   5. wrap   6. hire
7. paired   8. died

STORY #6: HARRIET TUBMAN (1820-1913); PAGE: 46

A. 1. They gave messages in the songs that they sang while working.   2. She would have blackouts or would fall asleep at any time or place during the day.   3. Answers will vary.   4. She softly sang 'When that chariot comes who's going with me?' outside the slaves cabins.
5. They sang back 'When that old chariot comes, I'm going with you.'   6. Someone may tell the overseer and she could be captured. Answers will vary.   7. Answers will vary.
B. 1. Some   2. others   3. One   4. Few   5. Each
C. Circled Words: afraid, unsafe, jumpy, irritated, nervous, insecure, frightened, unsure

STORY #7: EMILY PAULINE JOHNSON (1861-1913); PAGE: 48

A. 1. They lived in a beautiful mansion called 'Chiefswood.' They lived in luxury and met many important people. 2. Pauline attended parties, plays and she was a rich young woman. She spent time writing poetry. 3. George Johnson died and did not leave his family much money. Chiefswood had to be closed and the girls and their mother had to rent an apartment in Brantford. 4. She read her poetry at a recital and the audience loved it. 5. They had to travel by train or horse and wagon. They performed in town halls, saloons, schools, and church halls. 6. Pauline wore her native costume and told poems and stories about nature and Native People in Canada that the audience had never seen. 7. Flags were lowered in Vancouver, many people attended her funeral and her ashes were buried at Stanley Park where she would be close to nature.

B. 1. indefinite 2. personal 3. demonstrative 4. indefinite 5. interrogative 6. personal 7. interrogative 8. demonstrative 9. indefinite 10. personal

C. 1. party 2. write 3. govern 4. perform 5. press 6. poet 7. copy 8. clap 9. recite 10. forget

STORY #8: ROSE FORTUNE (1774-1864); PAGE: 50

A. 1. Answers will vary. 2. She transported luggage and goods in a wheelbarrow from ships to hotels or homes and gave wakeup calls to people who were travelling by ship or had appointments to go to. 3. She dressed in unusual clothes. She wore a dress with its petticoat showing, over it was an apron and a man's waistcoat. Her head was covered with a lace cap and over it sat a man's straw hat. She wore men's boots that had high heels and often carried a basket. 4. She discovered that teenage thugs were causing problems on the docks. 5. She attacked and spanked them. 6. She wanted to protect visitors and tourists who came by ship. 7. She took them from the docks to safe houses on the Underground Railway.

B. 1. ship sailed 2. Rose chased 3. wheelbarrow rolled 4. man caught 5. People stayed 6. Rose helped

C. 1. leaving, living, loyalist, luggage 2. carrier, caught, consider, curfew 3. waistcoat, warn, wharves, worn 4. thugs, transfer, transport, travelled 5. petticoat, problems, protect, provisions

STORY #9: SHAWNADITHIT (1800-1829); PAGE: 52

A. 1. The Europeans lured them on to their ships and sold them at slave markets. They feared the European guns. 2. They were starving to death, dying from European diseases or bring killed with guns. 3. The British had taken over their best hunting and fishing grounds. 4. She saw her mother and sister die. She found the dead bodies of her uncle and cousin. She was shot in the arm and foot by a trapper. She saw her father being chased by a man with a gun and watched him drown in an icy river. 5. William Cormack discovered she was the last Beothuk and wanted her to tell their history 6. She drew pictures of things her people used and maps. She taught him words in her language and told him about Beothuks' customs and beliefs. 7. Answers will vary.

B. 1. Beothuk, lived 2. British, settled 3. trapper, shot 4. men, captured 5. father, sank

C. 1. ar-rive 2. peo-ple 3. trap-per 4. set-tle-ment 5. hor-ror 6. star-va-tion 7. swir-ling 8. set-tlers 9. dis-ap-pear-ance 10. ar-tis-tic

STORY #10: MADELEINE JARRET TARIEU (1678-1774); PAGE: 54

A. 1. Possible answers: being attacked by wild animals; getting lost; cold weather; starvation; crop failures; wars; diseases 2. took command of the fort; shouted orders and pretended there were many soldiers inside; signalled for help by firing a canon; fought beside her brothers and a soldier; wore a soldier's hat; did not take time to eat or sleep; wouldn't let the cows in as Iroquois may be hiding under animal skins 3. Sequence Order: One day while working in a garden outside the fort, Madeleine saw an Iroquois approaching her. She quickly ran into the fort, closed the gate and began shouting orders. Donning a soldier's cap, Madeleine climbed up onto the stockade beside her brothers and the one soldier and prepared to shoot. When the others began shooting at the Iroquois, Madeleine fired off a canon to tell other forts they needed help. The next day help arrived and the prisoners held by the Iroquois were freed, the Iroquois had disappeared and the fort was saved.

B. Underlined word groups: 1. of Iroquois 2. about carefully and quietly 3. to use a gun properly 4. into the forest 5. by boat

C. 1. ai 2. ou 3. au 4. ea 5. oo 6. ou 7. ai 8. ea 9. oo 10. ai 11. ea 12. ou 13. ea 14. ui 15. ou

SSR1135 ISBN: 9781771589659
© On The Mark Press

Section 4
FAMOUS CANADIAN ATHLETES

STORY #1: SILKEN LAUMANN; PAGE: 56

A. 1. Number Order: 2, 1, 3, 4, 5, 3   2. Words will vary but must be appropriate.

B. 1. They, medal, sculls   2. Silken, it, she, her, leg
3. she, hospital, doctors, operations it   4. Atlanta, Silken, medal, sculls

C. 1. advanced   2. retired   3. capture   4. collided
5. exposed   6. endure   7. doomed   8. shone
9. selected   10. trained

STORY #2: HAYLEY WICKENHEISER; PAGE: 58

A. 1. to 5.   Answers will vary.

B. 1. past   2. present   3. past   4. future   5. present
6. future   7. past   8. past   9. present   10. present

C. 1. plural   2. possessive   3. plural   4. singular   5. plural
6. plural   7. possessive/plural   8. possessive/plural
9. plural   10. singular

STORY #3: JOANNIE ROCHETTE; PAGE: 60

A. Answers will vary in this section.

B. 1. past tense   2. present tense   3. future tense
4. past tense   5. future tense

C. 1. small   2. often   3. close   4. won   5. excellent
6. few   7. finished   8. leaving   9. alone   10. expensive

STORY #4: JENNIFER JONES; PAGE: 62

A. 1. When she was eleven, Jennifer's   2. Using strategy is an important   3. At the age of 16   4. This final shot was perfectly completed   5. Finally their chance came at
6. At the Olympics, Jennifer Jones   7. Team Canada won the finals   8. One of her big dreams

B. Underlined phrases: 1. to solve problems; at school
2. to watch; on the ice   3. At the 2013 Olympic Trials; to represent Canada; at the 2014 Sochi Olympics   4. After a loss; to quickly get back; to competing again

C. 1. career   2. difficult   3. major   4. compete   5. well known   6. tremendous   7. opportunity   8. tournament

STORY #5: KAILLIE HUMPHRIES; PAGE: 64

A. 1. 2007-2008   2. 2010   3. 2006-2007   4. 2008-2009
5. 2012   6. 2008-2009   7. 2006-2007   8. 2013

B. 1. down the track   2. of a bobsled team; down the course
3. of a team; down the icy course   4. of the fastest teams in the last run   5. In the closing ceremonies to carry Canada's flag

C. 1. competition   2. fortunately   3. elite   4. reunited
5. pilot   6. difficult   7. rookie   8. battled

STORY #6: TESSA VIRTUE/SCOTT MOIR; PAGE: 66

A. 1. Possible Answers: understanding, patient, friendship, competitive, committed, ambitious, passionate, agreeable, honourable, hard-working
2. strong dance skills, athletic, flexible, natural aptitude, good coordination, soft knees, rhythmical; expressive, similar bodies, good balance   3. Answers will vary.
4. Answers will vary.

B. 1. gracefully; adverb   2. coached; verb   3. cramps, pains; nouns   4. huge; adjective

C. 1. young   2. skate   3. province   4. compete   5. medal
6. fiddle   7. battle   8. win

STORY #7: ERIC LAMAZE; PAGE: 68

A. 1. Answers will vary.   2. Answers will vary.
3. Hickstead was a good jumper and had the same temperament as Lamaze.   4. It was the One Million CN International Competition   5. It was at the Bejing Olympic Games in 2008.   6. Hickstead dropped dead at an equestrian event in Italy.

B. 1. verb, phrase, pronoun, common noun   2. proper noun, verb, common noun, phrase   3. proper noun, proper noun, verb, common noun, verb, phrase, preposition

C. 1. positive   2. richest   3. heading   4. later
5. continued   6. weak

D. 1. opportunities   2. banned   3. collapsed   4. shocked
5. talent   6. immature

STORY #8 ALEXANDRE DESPATIE; PAGE: 70

A. 1. Sydney Olympic Games   2. 1998 Commonwealth Games   3. 2005 to 2007   4. before the Sydney Olympics in Australia   5. Beijing Olympics   6. before the London Olympics   7. Grand Prix Meet in Madrid, Spain   8. London Olympic Games

B. 1. proper noun, pronoun, verb, adjective   2. adjective, noun, verb, pronoun   3. adjective, noun, adjective, noun, verb, preposition, adjective   4. preposition, proper noun, verb, noun, adjective

C. 1. short a, long o   2. short e, long e   3. long e, long i
4. short i, long o   5. short a, long e   6. short a, short e, short i

STORY #9: STEVE NASH; PAGE 72

A. 1. his father played professional soccer.   2. Steve's father was finished playing professional soccer.
3. he was smaller and slimmer than most athletes.
4. he had achieved success in hockey even though he was smaller than other hockey players.   5. he was the worst defender that he had ever seen.   6. he would do anything to play on a professional basketball team
7. he received many different awards.   8. he has had many injuries that have prevented him from playing.

B. 1. proper noun, adjective, preposition, common noun
2. verb, pronoun, verb, common noun   3. common noun, verb, adjective, proper noun   4. verb, common noun, preposition, adjective, common noun

C. 1. skinny   2. excelled   3. participate   4. university
   5. graduated   6. shocked   7. traded   8. constantly

STORY #10: SYDNEY CROSBY; PAGE: 74

A. 1. Parents and players of opposing teams taunted and teased him; players on opposing teams tried to injure him on purpose; wouldn't wear his hockey jersey between games around people so they wouldn't know who he was.   2. They wanted him to improve and strengthen hockey skills; to help him to grow and mature as a person.   3. He became the youngest hockey player to become a captain of an NHL team   4. He had hits to his head in back-to-back games that caused a concussion and prevented him from playing
   5. Answers will vary.
B. 1. proper noun; verb; common noun; verb   2. verb; common noun; pronoun; phrase; phrase   3. adjective; common noun; verb; common noun; preposition; phrase
C. 1. minor (A)   2. league (S)   3. finish (S)
   4. strengthen (A)   5. physical (S)   6. same (A)
   7. special (A)   8. raised (A)

Section 5
FAMOUS CANADIAN INVENTORS AND INVENTIONS

STORY #1: THE DE HAVILLAND BEAVER; PAGE: 76

A. 1. The Beaver   2. The Otter   3. The Twin Otter
   4. The Twin Otter   5. The Otter   6. The Twin Otter
   7. The Beaver   8. The Otter
B. Answers will vary.
C. 1. pontoons   2. Beaver   3. areas   4. heavy   5. jeep
   6. aircraft   7. clear   8. needed   9. built   10. tough
   11. wheels   12. quieter   13. terrain   14. features
   15. around   16. mountains   17. balloon   18. ground

STORY #2: THE TRANS-CANADA HIGHWAY; PAGE: 78

A. 1. asphalt, Newfoundland, Victoria   2. 7 821, barren, cities, mountains   3. cross, territories   4. province, cost, part, highway   5. blasted, clear, bridges, rivers, streams   6. green, white, leaf, logo   7. declared, Labour, Prime
B. 1. long, winding, lazily, crystal, clear, tall, bubbly
   2. slowly, rugged,   3. road, carefully, huge   4. large, eventually, fast-flowing, wide
C. Three Syllable Words; continent; national; scenery; Newfoundland; Atlantic, provinces; construction; parliament; dangerous; bicycles   Four Syllable Words: transportation; spectacular; interesting; territories; responsible; economy; motorcycles; delivering; Diefenbaker

STORY #3: THE WORLD'S TALLEST TOTEM POLE; PAGE: 80

A. 1. False   2. True   3. False   4. True   5. False   6. False
   7. False   8. True
B 1. adverb phrase: at a young age   2. adjective phrase: in the world; adverb phrase: in British Columbia
   3. adjective phrase: of great size; adverb phrase: to make totem poles   4. adverb phrase: at its front door
   5. adjective phrase: of birds and animals; adverb phrase: on the totem poles
C. 1. tr   2. kn   3. sw   4. sk   5. fr   6. cl   7. gr   8. st
   9. gr   10. st   11. cr   12. th   13. bl   14. wh   15. str
   16. sh   17. sh   18. th   19. br   20. ch   21. gr   22. st
   23. br   24. ch

STORY #4: THE INVENTOR OF INSULIN; PAGE: 82

A. 1. One of his friends named Jane died from it at the age of 14.   2. He was interested in a gland called the pancreas found behind the stomach.   3. The pancreas treats the protein, starch, and fats that we take into our bodies so they can be used the best possible way.   4. It is a disease that causes the oversupply of sugar in the blood.   5. They tried it on a fourteen year old boy who was dying from diabetes and he recovered.
   6. It is made from the glands of cows being slaughtered for markets.
B 1. adjective   2. adverb   3. adjective, adverb, adverb
   4. adverb, adjective
C. 1. names, named, naming   2. dies, dying, died
   3. confuses, confusing confused   4. shrivels shrivelled, shrivelling   5. hopes, hoped, hoping   6. regulates, regulated, regulating

STORY #5: NEW TOOLS TO PERFORM BODY FUNCTIONS; PAGE: 84

A. Sequential Ordering: 4, 6, 1, 5, 8, 2, 7, 3
B Underlined words: 1. lost, leg   2. replaced, hands
   3. powered, body   4. becoming, popular
C. 1. baby   2. elect   3. skill   4. fit   5. measure
   6. amputate   7. plant   8. form   9. able   10. control

Section 6
FAMOUS CANADIAN ANIMALS

STORY #1: WORLD WAR I HORSES; PAGE: 86

A. 1. The men could not charge and shoot at the men in the trenches and too many men died.   2. They were needed to pull wagons, guns, and equipment.   3. Baker was going to fight with his men in the trenches and Morning Glory and all the other horses were sent to France   4. Lt. Col. Baker was killed on June 2, in 1916.   5. She did not have to pull heavy loads because she was used as a personal mount by a battalion commander.

 SSR1135   ISBN: 9781771589659
© On The Mark Press

B 1. B. S. world; B. P. was involved; O. war   2. B. S. soldiers; B. P. fought; O. trenches   3. B. S. horses; B. P. walked; O. places   4. B. S. Morning Glory B. P. was loved; O. people

C. 1. cavalry   2. trench   3. charge   4. volunteer   5. fortunate   6. battalion

STORY #2: BIG BEN; PAGE: 88

A. 1. Answers will vary.   2. Answers will vary.   3. They won many competitions and earned a great deal of money.   4. They won at Spruce Meadows and had three more Grand Prix Wins.   5. It was an incredible feat for a horse to compete at such a high level after having two colic surgeries.   6. He was involved in a bad highway accident while travelling with other horses in a trailer to a show.

B. 1. B. S. Big Ben; B. P. spent; O. winters   2. B. S. Millar; B. P. went; O. horse   3. B. S. horse; B. P. was born; O. farm   4. B. S. Millar and Ben   B. P. made; O. team

C. 1. famous   2. purchased   3. talented   4. bond   5. colic   6. ovation   7. euthanize   8. audience

STORY #3 THE NEWFOUNDLAND DOG; PAGE: 90

A. 1. it can swim through rough waves in the ocean.   2. it can swim long distances in very cold water.   3. it can swim long distances.   4. can walk over sandy shores and marshes.   5. as working dogs to help fishermen on their boats.   6. to pull carts and carry packs on its back.   7. it is intelligent, loyal, and calm.   8. they rescue people in ocean waters.

B 1. Proper Noun; adjective; common noun   2. adjective; adverb; preposition; noun; adjective   3. verb; preposition; noun; verb; noun   4. Proper noun; noun; preposition

C. 1. large   2. loyal   3. rare   4. able   5. fortune   6. marsh   7. story   8. own   9. slip   10. struggle

Section 7
FAMOUS CANADIAN ATTRACTIONS

STORY #1: PERCÉ ROCK; PAGE: 92

A. Sequential Ordering: 5, 8, 1, 4, 6, 3, 7, 2

B. 1. sailed, quickly   2. walked, carefully   3. slapped, very, hard   4. Extremely, rough   5. suddenly, jumped

C. 1. celebrations, apparition, gradually, peninsula, spectacular   2. a) journey; b) huge; c) apparition; d) massive; e) visable; f) suddenly; g) avoid; h) appearance; i) types; j) connects

STORY #2: NIAGARA FALLS; PAGE: 94

A. 1. (5) The three waterfalls form   2. (7) The three falls were formed   3. (2) There are three waterfalls   4. (2) There are three waterfalls   5. (3) The Horseshoe Falls is   6. (4) The three waterfalls straddle   7. (1) It is one of   8. (12) Many daredevils have tried

B. 1. The three falls are called the Horseshoe Falls, the American Falls, and the Bridal Falls.   2. People travel between Canada and the United States on the Rainbow Bridge.   3. Did you know Niagara Falls got its name from a Mohawk word?

C. 1. waterfalls, horseshoe, rainbow, daredevils, tightrope, downstream, without   2. falls, smaller, smallest, straddle, waterfalls, carries, barrels, across, crossed   3. a) over; b) back; c) heavier; d) louder; e) beautiful, colder; g) long; h) top; i) near; j) more

STORY #3: HOODOOS AND THE ALBERTA BADLANDS; PAGE: 96

A. 1. False   2. True   3. True   4. True   5. False   6. True   7. False   8. False

B 1. and   2. or   3. but   4. and

C. 1. hoof   2. zoom   3. brook   4. crook   5. spooky   6. igloo   7. moose   8. spoon

STORY #4: THE RIDEAU CANAL; PAGE: 98

A. 1. military purposes; communications; to ship logs, timber, minerals, grains; travel route for British settlers.   2. pleasure boating, boat tours, skating   3. It took six years. Everything would have to be done by hand as there were no machines.   4. Thousands of Irish and French-Canadian labourers   5. They died from malaria, other diseases, and accidents   6. Canada and the United States were at peace

B. Underlined words: 1. labourers, maleria, diseases, accidents   2. were shipped   3. main, travel, British   4. slowly, steadily

C. 1. plan   2. invade   3. use   4. settle   5. operate   6. large   7. attract   8. labour   9. serve   10. communicate

STORY #5: QUÉBEC CITY; PAGE: 100

A. 1. It is located on top of a cliff overlooking the St. Lawrence River.   2. It has a wall around it.   3. It comes from the Algonquian word 'kebec' and it means narrowing of the water.   4. It is the Château Frontenac.   5. They are connected by 30 sets of stairs and a funicular.   6. The battle took place on the Plains of Abraham.   7. It is the Sainte-Anne-de-Beaupre Shrine.

B. 1. nouns   2. adjectives   3. adverbs   4. adjectives   5. verbs

C. 1. site   2. oldest   3. narrowing   4. stairs   5. plains   6. near   7. tallest   8. led   9. won   10. interesting   11. battle   12. harbour

STORY #6: THE R.C.M.P. ACADEMY AND HERITAGE CENTRE; PAGE: 102

A. 1. It was needed to bring law and order, to drive out whisky traders and outlaws, and to have peace with the First Nation people.   2. He rode into a Sioux camp of 5000 warriors and told Sitting Bull, their chief, that he and his men had to obey Canada's laws.   3. It trains young people to be officers in the R.C.M.P.   4. It has many artifacts used by the R.C.M.P. in the past.   5. old equipment, weapons, uniforms, photographs on display, clothing, Louis Riel's handcuffs and crucifix, a spy's uniform, chemical-tipped matches, pen microphone, gifts from Sitting Bull, snowshoes of Mad Trapper   6. They are the Sergeant Major's Parade and the Sunset Retreat Ceremony.

B. 1. Underline: to bring and order; to the west; Circle: law, order, west   2. Underline: to bagpipe music; of a snare drum; Circle: music, drum   3. Underline: In one display; of a spy; Circle: display; spy   4. Underline: to Canada; to hide; from the American cavalry   Circle: Canada, hide; cavalry

C. 1. the killing of people and animals for no reason   2. to set up, to settle   3. dealings between people, groups, countries   4. something made by people such as a weapon or tool   5. make a picture of   6. based on history   7. a place where people are hanged   8. to mix together

STORY #7: A MENNONITE HERITAGE VILLAGE; PAGE: 104

A. 1. Answers will vary.   2. built shelters out of sod; introduced fruit trees, sunflowers, watermelons; built windmills and steam mills to grind wheat into flour for Canada and other countries; grew wheat in large fields.   3. Answers will vary.   4. Checkmarks should be beside: milking a cow; churning cream into butter; spinning wool into yarn; making wax candles; weaving on a loom; grinding wheat into flour; sewing on a quilt; making bread

B. Sentences will vary.

C. 1. (H)   2. (A)   3. (S)   4. (A)   5. (A)   6. (H)   7. (H)   8. (S)   9. (A)

STORY #8: FORT HENRY, KINGSTON: A POPULAR MILITARY MUSEUM; PAGE: 106

A. 1. The Ante Room   2. Bakery   3. Soldier's Barracks   4. Officer's Barracks   5. school   6. The Powder Magazine   7. Garrison Cells   8. Married-Quarters

B. Paragraphs will vary.

C. 1. barracks   2. cannon   3. officers   4. battery   5. garrison   6. shuttered   7. drills   8. battle

Section 8
FAMOUS CANADIAN FESTIVALS

STORY #1: THE CALGARY STAMPEDE; PAGE: 108

A. Answers will vary.

B. Paragraphs will vary.

C. 1. rodeo   2. parade   3. midway   4. stampede   5. bareback   6. concerts   7. horses   8. cowboys   9. prairie   10. pemmican   11. famous   12. compete

STORY #2: THE QUÉBEC WINTER CARNIVAL; PAGE: 110

A. 1. It is held in mid-January to mid-February in Québec City.   2. It has been taking place for 56 years.   3. Bonhomme is the guest of honour and mascot.   4. It is the Ice Palace.   5. horse drawn sleigh racing, canoe racing, dogsled racing   6. One takes place during the day and one takes place at night.   7. They like to eat maple sugar and beavertails.

B. Paragraphs will vary.

C. 1. winter   2. largest   3. day   4. smile   5. leading   6. high   7. pulling   8. fastest   9. floating   10. hardens

STORY #3: THE SANTA CLAUS PARADE; PAGE: 112

A. 1. 1919   2. 1982   3. 1917   4. 1906   5. 2004   6. 1952   7. 1913   8. 1951

B. Answers will vary.

C. 1. real   2. eight   3. plane   4. different   5. hurried   6. arrived   7. route   8. filled   9. longer   10. drawn

Photo credits: Neftali / Shutterstock.com
TradingCardsNPS / Flickr
Louis-Philippe Hébert Jeangagnon via Wikimedia Commons

SSR1135   ISBN: 9781771589659
© On The Mark Press